Behold Your Mother
Woman of Faith

A Pastoral Letter
on the
Blessed Virgin Mary

November 21, 1973
National Conference of Catholic Bishops

© Copyright 1973
United States Catholic Conference
1312 Massachusetts Avenue, N.W.
Washington, D.C. 20005
All rights reserved.

Analytical Table of Contents

INTRODUCTION 1

I. OUR LADY IN THE BIBLE 5

    Great women of the Old Testament 5
    People of Israel as "Bride of Yahweh," "Daughter of Zion" 5
    Eve and Mary 5
    Mary in the Gospel of St. Luke 6
    Zephaniah's Anticipation of Gabriel's Message 8
    Nathan Tells David of Jesus' Coming 8
    Mary's Child the "Son of God" 9
    The Ark of the Covenant and Mary 9
    Mary and Abraham 11
    Mary and Elizabeth 12
    Mary in the Gospel of St. John 12
        Mary at Cana and at Calvary 12

II. THE CHURCH'S UNDERSTANDING OF THE MYSTERY OF MARY 15

    Seeing Mary in the Scriptures 15
    The New Eve 15
    The Virginal Conception 16
        The Church's Constant Teaching 16
        The Creeds 17
        Mary's Virginity in the 2d Century Fathers 17
        The Precursors of Jesus: Isaac, Samuel, John the Baptist 18
    Mary Always a Virgin 19
        St. Jerome and the "Brothers of the Lord" 19
    The Blessedness of Mary 20
        The Immaculate Conception 20
        The Assumption 22
    Mary, Mother of God—*Theotokos* 23

III. MARY, MEDIATRIX AND SPIRITUAL MOTHER 25
    Vatican II and the Title "Mediatrix" 25
    Mary's Role as Mediatrix 25
    Mary as Spiritual Mother 27
        Mother of the Church 27
        Mother of the Members of Christ 27
        The Faithful Christian as Mother of Christ 27
        Mary, Mother of the Spiritual Life 27

IV. MARY IN OUR LIFE 31
    Mary as Intercessor 31
    Mary in the Communion of Saints 31
    Mary in the Mass 32
    Mary and Those Who Have Died in Christ 33
    Mary in the Eastern Rites 34
    Mary in Christian Devotion 34
        Decline of Marian Devotion Today 34
        Mary in the Liturgy 35
        Extra-liturgical devotions 36
        The Rosary 36
        Apparitions of the BVM—Lourdes, LaSalette,
          Fatima, Guadalupe 37
    Mary and Ecumenism 38
        The Reformation 39
        Vatican II on the Hierarchy of Truths 40
        Tradition and the Magisterium 41

V. MARY, MOTHER OF THE CHURCH 43
    Pope Paul's Use of the Title 43
    Mary and the Holy Spirit 44
    Mary and the Priesthood 44
    Mary and the Religious Life 45
    Mary and Family Life 47
        Reverence for Human Life 48
        Christian Marriage 48
        The Christian Home 49
          The Prayer Life of the Home 50
    Mary and the Dignity of Women 50
    Mary and Youth 51
    Mary and Single Life in the World 51

CONCLUSION 52

APPENDIX—MARY'S PLACE IN AMERICAN CATHOLIC
  HISTORY 53

REFERENCES 56

SUGGESTED READINGS 59

STUDY QUESTIONS 61

INTRODUCTION

Dearly Beloved:

1 We your Bishops and your brothers in the faith, are addressing to you a Pastoral Letter on the Blessed Virgin Mary. We wish to share with you our faith in the truths concerning her and together with you to express publicly our filial love for her. The Gospels summon us all to recognize the special place the Mother of Jesus has in God's plan for the salvation of mankind. The teachings of Popes and Councils lead us to an ever clearer understanding of Mary's privileged position in the Church. Singular honor has been given her in piety, art, music and literature. Surely this Catholic tradition is a fulfillment of her prophecy: "All ages to come shall call me blessed" (Lk. 1:48).

2 In order to serve better the current needs of men, the Church seeks to adapt herself to the widespread social and cultural changes of our time. Nevertheless, under the guidance of the Holy Spirit, she must preserve intact the divine message which she has received from Christ. This includes the special role of Mary in the mystery of the salvation of the human race. Through this letter we hope to reaffirm our heritage of faith in Mary, the Mother of God, and to encourage authentic devotion to her.

3 First of all, we should clearly understand that the Second Vatican Council in no way downgraded faith in or devotion to Mary. On the contrary, the eighth chapter of the Constitution on the Church is a clear and penetrating account of Catholic teaching on the Blessed Mother of God. Other ages have erected shrines and temples in her honor. This chapter, fashioned from the inspired texts of Sacred Scripture, the teachings of early Christian writers, and the practice and prayer life of the Church, is in reality a beautiful spiritual shrine in which the Mother of Jesus is honored and from which she continues to speak to us with a mother's loving concern. Our Holy Father, Pope Paul VI, has repeatedly affirmed the position of the Council. He called the chapter on Our Lady "a vast synthesis of Catholic doctrine" concerning her place in the mystery of Christ and his Church. He also recalled that she was the heavenly patroness to whom Pope John entrusted the Council.[1]

4 These words of ours are the preamble to our full Pastoral Letter on Our Lady. We have called upon dedicated theologians to aid us in restating the teachings of the Church about her. Here again the Council documents have guided our approach. We hope and pray that our presentation will be a subject for serious study and loving reflection. We desire with all our hearts that it be received into homes and rectories and seminaries, into schools and institutes of higher learning, into adult education groups, confraternity centers, campus ministries and religious communities.

5 The intercession of Mary extends not only to individuals but to the whole community of believers. She has a place in the ongoing work of redemption, which has as its goal, "to bring all things in the heavens and on earth into one under Christ's headship" (Eph. 1:10). The full sense of Mary's role is summed up in the title Pope Paul gave her, "Mother of the Church."[2] Because of her divine maternity, Mary stands in a unique relationship with her Savior and her Son. "Believing and obeying, she brought forth on earth the Father's Son . . . whom God placed as the first-born among many brethren, namely, the faithful. In their birth and development she cooperates with a maternal love."[3]

6 Sometimes anxiety is expressed that devotion to Mary may detract from the position of Jesus, our one Lord and Mediator. Such fear is unfounded. The more we know and love Mary, the more surely will we know and love Jesus and understand His mission in the world. It is also true that the more we know Jesus and love Him, the better we will appreciate His Mother's place in God's plan for man's redemption. This is the teaching of the Second Vatican Council. Her motherly intercession, the Council made clear, in no way diminishes the unique mediation of Christ, but rather shows its power. God's free choice is the reason for Mary's place in the plan for our redemption. She is totally dependent on her son. Commenting on the words of the Council, Paul VI declared: "Devotion to the Virgin Mother of God does not stop with her, but has to be regarded as a help which of its very nature leads men to Christ."[4]

7 Dearly beloved brothers and sisters, this is the faith we share with you:

8 We honor Mary as the Mother of Jesus Christ, the Incarnate Word of God. We recognize her unique and exalted role in the redemption her Son brought to men. We love Mary. We try to imitate her virtues of faith, purity, humility and conformity to the will of God, which are part of the very texture of the Gospel message.

9 We acknowledge that devotion to Mary, the joyful duty of all of us, has a special function in exalting the dignity of woman and fostering respect for her person. We believe in the power of Mary's intercession to bring us, as individuals and as a community, under the influence of Christ's redeeming mercy.

10 With all the affection of our hearts and the full submission of our minds to the truths of our holy Faith, we repeat the Church's familiar words in praise of the Mother of Jesus:

> Blessed be the great Mother of God, Mary most holy.
> Blessed be her holy and Immaculate Conception.
> Blessed be her glorious Assumption.
> Blessed be the name of Mary, Virgin and Mother.

11 United with our Holy Father, we proclaim once more the preeminent position of Mary in "the mystery of Christ and the Church." We urge the restoration and renewal of the ancient love of Christendom for the Mother of the Lord as a tribute to lay tenderly at her feet. In this Holy Year, we pray that she may fill the hearts of all men with peace and lead them to know and love Jesus Christ, her Son, and to share in the abundant fruits of His redemption.

Chapter One
OUR LADY IN THE BIBLE

12 The Holy Spirit led the Second Vatican Council to describe our Lady's life on earth as a pilgrimage of faith.[1] This approach to the Virgin Mary based on the Bible is especially suited to the needs of our day. Remembering the coming of the Son of God among us as the Son of Mary, in one of the earliest New Testament passages, St. Paul wrote: "When the designated time had come, God sent forth his Son born of a woman, born under the law." According to the plan of the Father of mercies this took place "that we might receive the adoption of sons" (Gal 4:4-5). Following St. Paul, the evangelists portrayed the special significance of the Virgin Mary. St. Luke's Annunciation narrative stands in the tradition of Old Testament announcements delivered by angels, in which God chose men to play a special part in the messianic preparations.

13 In the history of Israel, women as well as men had privileged roles in the accomplishment of God's saving plan. The Old Testament shows a line of great men of the Bible as "standard-bearers" of redemption: Adam, Abraham, Moses and others; and a parallel line of believers in the saving action of the Lord, the great women: Eve, Sarah, Miriam, and even the whole people of Israel under a feminine image "bride of Yahweh," "Daughter of Zion."

14 The future Eve, to whose offspring victory over Satan is promised, is realized in the great Old Testament women, but preeminently in Mary of Nazareth, whose obedient expression of faith, "Let it be done to me as you say" (Lk 1:38), heals the disobedience of the first Eve. The comparison between the first Eve, primitive mother of the living, and Mary, the new Eve, is the oldest Christian reflection on the Blessed Virgin outside the Bible, and accords well with the New Testament teaching that Christ is the new Adam (Rom 5:19).

15 The Eve-Mary comparison is rooted in the covenant theology of the Old Testament, in which God's free initiative stirs up man's response of faith. Faith, God's gift, becoming then truly man's possession, marks the moment when mankind receives salvation. In Mary's response, "Let it be done to me as you say," the expectation of the old covenant achieves perfect expression. God bestows His grace freely. He chose Mary, prepared her, guided her to a fully human consent. Mary, then, has a central function in the fulfillment of redemption. Her faith opened the way for Jesus to perform His salvific mission. God's free election made Mary the representative of the believing remnant. In the Council's words, "She stands out among the poor and humble of the Lord who confidently await and receive salvation from Him" (n. 55). Mary is the "exalted Daughter of Zion" in whom, after the long waiting for the promise, the times are fulfilled and the new dispensation is established. "All this occurred when the Son of God took a human nature from her, that He might in the mysteries of His flesh free man from sin." [2]

16 The designation "Daughter of Zion," evocative of Mt. Zion and the temple, is used in the Old Testament for the messianic community, especially that remnant of the chosen people who returned to Jerusalem after the Exile. "Daughter of Zion" includes "the poor and lowly," the humble of spirit, the devout believers who counted on God for salvation.

The Gospel of St. Luke

17 Luke begins his gospel by taking us into the company of poor and holy people: Elizabeth and Zachary, Anna and Simeon, Joseph and Mary. Jesus himself and the Good News came from this circle, cradle of the Christian Church. For St. Luke, Mary is the perfect example of awaiting the Messiah with a pure and humble spirit. Luke sees in Mary the Daughter of Zion who rejoices because God is with her and who praises His greatness for pulling down the mighty and exalting the humble.

18 God's guidance of His people of Israel culminated in the exemplary role of the "Daughter of Zion" who was to give the world the universal Redeemer. God's favor was expressed in the initial gift of grace to Mary which we call the "Immaculate Conception." Mary was the person who acted on behalf of "the total remnant"; she stood out among the Lord's poor and lowly who looked for salvation. Kept free from original sin, she was able to give herself wholeheartedly to the saving work of her Son. By accepting the Annunciation, she became intimately associated with all the saving mysteries of Jesus' life, death, and Resurrection. "Just as a woman contributed to death, so also a woman should contribute to life." [3]

19 Even the books of the Old Testament, as they are understood by the Church in the light of Christian revelation, "bring the figure of the woman, Mother of the Redeemer, into a gradually sharper focus" (n. 55). In the fulfillment, we find the vague "figure of a woman" realized in *the* woman who is Mary of Nazareth, the "predestined mother" who would not merely "contribute to life" but bring into the world the One who is Life itself and who renews all things.[4] The light of completion shows that the Redeemer's Mother was "already prophetically foreshadowed in that victory over the serpent which was promised to our first parents after their fall into sin (cf. Gen 3:15)."[5] With St. Matthew, the Church holds that the Mother of Jesus is likewise the Virgin who will conceive a Son called Emmanuel (Mt 1:22-23, cf. Is 7:14, Mi 5:2-3).

20 The bridge-role of Mary between the Old Testament and New, between expectation and fulfillment, appears not only in individual texts, such as St. Matthew's use of Isaiah, but is an integral element of the Gospel view of Mary. For St. Luke and St. John the Mother of Jesus is the typical, the perfect believer. The "handmaid of the Lord" in St. Luke's infancy chapters, and the "woman" in St. John's Cana and Calvary narratives is at once the individual "Daughter of Zion," in whom Old Testament hopes are achieved, and the type of the Church, Bride of Christ, new mother of all men. The primitive Church saw in Mary the fulfillment and personification of the Church, Mother of the messianic people.

21 Thanks to the recent researches of scholars, we have become aware of new depths in the Gospel portrait of Mary. In the past, as in the image of the "Daughter of Zion," the liturgy, both for Advent and the Immaculate Conception, has, in fact, incorporated such texts long before their scientific exposition. The Holy Spirit leads the Christian people in many ways. The celebration of the mystery of Mary in the liturgy and other prayer is a school of the faith and a profession of doctrine.

22 Under the inspiration of the Holy Spirit, the early Church had long reflected on Jesus, who He was and why He had come, before any book of the New Testament was written. A rich "allusive theology" is characteristic of the first two chapters, the most mature section, of St. Luke's gospel. The author went back to the Old Testament for words and phrases to describe New Testament events. By multiple allusions to the Old Testament, St. Luke shows Jesus as the promised Messiah. These allusions can be illustrated here by a summary of the Annunciation story. The opening words of Gabriel, best known as the beginning of the "Hail Mary," repeat the promise of hope that the prophet Zephaniah addressed to his people ("Daughter of Zion") as they faced the threat of invasion 625 years before Christ:

> "Shout for joy, O daughter Zion!
> sing joyfully, O Israel!
> Be glad and exult with all your heart,
> O daughter Jerusalem!
> The Lord has removed the judgment against you,
> he has turned away your enemies;
> The King of Israel, the Lord, is in your midst,
> you have no further misfortune to fear.
> On that day, it shall be said to Jerusalem:
> Fear not, O Zion, be not discouraged!
> The Lord, your God, is in your midst,
> a mighty savior;
> He will rejoice over you with gladness,
> and renew you in his love,
> He will sing joyfully because of you," (Zep 3:14-17).

23 The pattern of allusions to the Old Testament continues as Gabriel speaks of the place of Jesus among the descendants of David, and then of the divinity of the Son of Mary. The Old Testament counterpart to the angelic words about the relationship of Jesus to royal David and His eternal rule over the house of Jacob is the prophecy of Nathan addressed to King David a thousand years before: "And when your time comes and you rest with your ancestors, I will raise up your heir after you, sprung from your loins, and I will make his kingdom firm. It is he who shall build a house for my name. And I will make his royal throne firm forever. I will be a father to him, and he shall be a son to me. And if he does wrong, I will correct him with the rod of men and with human chastisements; but I will not withdraw my favor from him as I withdrew it from your predecessor Saul, whom I removed from my presence. Your house and your kingdom shall endure forever before me; your throne shall stand firm forever" (2 Sm 7:12-16).

24 In St. Luke's beautifully balanced story, our Lady's words come next: "How can this be since I do not know man?" Mary's question is evidence of the belief of the early Church that Jesus was virginally conceived, the doctrine usually called the "Virgin Birth." Gabriel's reply to Mary's question leads into the second main part of his message: that the holy Child to be born of Mary will be not only the promised Messiah, but God made man. The angel explains the virginal conception of Jesus as being due to the power of God who has chosen this unique way to send His Son among men as their true brother and Savior. In Jesus, mankind gets a fresh start. The conception of the Son of Mary without a human father is the sign that the Incarnation is the new creation, independent of the will of man or urge of the flesh (Jn 1:13). The merciful Father intervenes in human history to send the new Adam, born of the Virgin Mary through the power of the Spirit.

25 "Hence, the holy offspring to be born will be called Son of God" (Lk 1:35). The title "Son of God" provides solid ground for us to profess our faith in the divinity of Jesus. Yet Gabriel's words offer an even more subtle and profound reason for affirming that the Son of Mary is truly the Son of God, Emmanuel, God-with-us. Again the key is found in the Old Testament. When the Israelites were wandering through the desert they carried with them the precious "ark of the covenant," a chest made of wood, containing the tables of the law, Aaron's rod, and other sacred objects. They called it "of the covenant" because it reminded them of the alliance between God and Israel. They believed that where the ark of the covenant was, the invisible God was present in a special way. Above the ark and the tent containing it, an overshadowing cloud was the visible sign of God's invisible presence. When the temple was built by Solomon, the ark of the covenant was placed in the Holy of Holies and remained the center of worship and sacrifice. After Jerusalem fell to the

Babylonian army in 587 B.C., the ark disappeared and has never been found. But its memory still serves Jew and Christian as a symbol of God's protecting presence.

26 One of the many descriptions of the ark and the overshadowing cloud is found in Exodus 40:

> "Moses did exactly as the Lord commanded him. On the first day of the first month of the second year the Dwelling was erected. It was Moses who erected the Dwelling. . . . He took the commandments and put them in the ark; . . . He brought the ark into the Dwelling . . . Then the cloud covered the meeting tent, and the glory of the Lord filled the Dwelling. Moses could not enter the meeting tent, because the cloud settled down upon it and the glory of the Lord filled the Dwelling" (Ex 40:16-21 and 34-35).

27 The ark of the covenant and the covering cloud influence St. Luke's narrative. In his account, however, the vivifying power of the unseen Spirit overshadows the Virgin, and God is made visibly present as the Son of Mary. The Mother of Jesus is the new and perfect ark of the covenant, the living tabernacle of the divine presence. The sacred ark that disappeared six centuries before has now returned in a more perfect way. Mary is the living ark of the covenant carrying Jesus. Salvation comes through Mary's flesh, through Mary's faith.

The "ark of the covenant" theme continues in St. Luke's account of Mary's visit to her cousin, Elizabeth. The Old Testament counterpart is provided by the story of the transfer of the ark of the covenant by King David (2 Sm 6). Without elaborating details, we suggest here the parallels between Lk 1 and 2 Sm 6:

a) David dances for joy before the ark. —The unborn John the Baptist leaps for joy in Elizabeth's womb.

b) David calls out: "How can the ark of the Lord come to me?" —Elizabeth cries out: "Who am I that the mother of my Lord should come to me?"

> David's cry of reverential fear was prompted by the sudden death of Uzzah, who had dared to touch the ark; that note of terror is totally absent in the joyous response of Elizabeth.

c) "The ark of the Lord remained in the house of Obed-edom the Gittite for three months, and the Lord blessed Obed-edom and his whole house." —As St. Luke tells it, Mary remained "about three months" and clearly Zachary's whole house received great blessing from the presence of Mary's unborn Son.

28 The episode of the Annunciation concludes with a double tribute to Mary's faith. The better-known is Mary's word of consent; her maternal "yes" was also her act of faith: "I am the servant of the Lord. Let it be done to me as you say" (Lk 1:38). These words have echoed and re-echoed in Christian liturgy and literature from earliest times. The chapter on Mary in the Dogmatic Constitution on the Church may be regarded as an extended commentary on her consent at the Annunciation. The opening sentence of n. 53 is typical: "At the message of the angel, the Virgin Mary received the Word of God into her heart and her body, and gave Life to the world."[6]

29 Less well known is the delicate praise of Mary's faith embodied in the final words of Gabriel: "for nothing is impossible with God" (Lk 1:37). This phrase is taken from the Genesis story of Abraham, great Old Testament "man of faith." For Christians, too, Abraham is "our father in faith," as we still call him in Eucharistic Prayer I. The memory of Abraham permeates the opening chapters of St. Luke, as it does the epistles to the Romans, the Galatians and the Hebrews, and his name and faith are commemorated repeatedly in Christian liturgical prayer.

30 There are remarkable likenesses between Abraham and Mary, especially in the accounts of the birth of Isaac, child of promise, and the virginal conception of Jesus, holy Child of Mary. Abraham, Old Testament man of faith, illuminates our understanding of Mary, New Testament woman of faith. Abraham, our father in faith, can teach us much about Mary, our mother in faith.

31 Mary's "song of poverty," the *Magnificat,* concludes: "He has upheld Israel his servant ever mindful of his mercy; even as he promised our fathers, promised Abraham and his descendants forever" (Lk 1:54-55).

32 Genesis relates the dramatic story of the son whom God sent to Abraham and Sarah in their old age. In this son, Isaac, all nations will be blessed. Even when Abraham is preparing to sacrifice his child, he still believes that somehow God's promise will be fulfilled. St. Paul reflects: "He is father of us all . . . in the sight of God in whom he believed, the God who restores the dead to life and calls into being those things which had not been. Hoping against hope, Abraham believed. . . . Without growing weak in faith, he thought of his own body . . . and of the dead womb of Sarah. Yet he never questioned or doubted God's promise; rather, he was strengthened in faith and gave glory to God, fully persuaded that God could do whatever he had promised" (Rom 4:16-21). When Abraham was told that Isaac was to be born, God strengthened him with the reminder that all things are possible to God (Gen 18:14). That divine reminder runs like a refrain through the many references to Abraham in both Testaments. Sometimes the words are declarative: "All things are possible to God." At other times they form a rhetorical question: "Is there anything God cannot do?" Still again, the divine assurance is simply alluded to: "fully persuaded that God could do whatever he had promised" (Rom 4:21).

33 Gabriel concludes his message with the unexpected news of Elizabeth's pregnancy, and then repeats the powerful words associated with Abraham in Genesis: "for nothing is impossible with God" (Lk 1:37). St. Luke places Mary, daughter of Abraham, before us as the great Gospel model of faith. He applies to her virginal motherhood the promise made to Abraham, remote ancestor of the Messiah. In the strength of her faith, Mary consents to the merciful Father's invitation, and in the power of the Spirit becomes the Mother of Jesus, Son of God in human flesh.

The Gospel of St. John

34 In the gospel of St. John, the Mother of Jesus appears at Cana and Calvary, the beginning and the end of her Son's public life. Both times Jesus addresses her as "woman." Each scene turns on a special "hour." At Cana, the hour refers to the beginning of the messianic ministry that "has not yet come" (Jn 2:4), yet which commences in "this first of his signs" that Jesus worked at Mary's request. At Calvary, we have the arrival of the great Johannine hour when Jesus "will be lifted up and draw all men" to himself (Jn 12:32). It is moreover "on the third day" that the wedding feast takes place, and "the third day" is the fulfillment of the sacred time of the paschal mystery. What began at Cana achieved its consummation on Calvary.

35 The words of Jesus to His Mother, "Woman, how does this concern of yours involve me? My hour has not yet come," (Jn 2:4) were an invitation to deepen her faith, to look beyond the failing wine to His messianic career. At the close of the Cana narrative, St. John tells its purpose: "Jesus performed this first of his signs. . . . Thus did he reveal his glory and his disciples believed in him" (Jn 2:11). For St. John, the signs (or miracles) of Jesus always have to do with the awakening or strengthening of the faith of His followers. It is striking that no sign is done to help Mary believe. The Mother of Jesus requires no miracle to strengthen her faith. At her Son's word, before "this first of his signs," she shows her faith.

36 Mary's presence at the wedding feast reveals much about her. We see her quick grasp of the situation, her concern over the embarrassment of the young couple, her willingness to make compassionate intercession. "She was moved by pity, and her intercession brought about the beginning of miracles by Jesus the Messiah."[7] The significance of Mary is also richly ecclesial. At first, Mary is the figure of the synagogue, Daughter of Zion of old, still making use of the imperfect means of the past, the water in the stone jars "as prescribed for Jewish ceremonial washings." But when she says to the waiters, "Do whatever he tells you" (Jn 2:5), she becomes the figure of the new People of God. The change of water into abundant and very good wine symbolizes the coming of messianic times. Mary is present as figure of the Church, Bride of Christ. On behalf of the Church she greets the messianic Bridegroom. At her request the new wine is supplied.

37 The meaning of Mary at Cana is revealed fully when His Mother stands "near the cross of Jesus," and hears Him say: "Woman, there is your Son" (Jn 19:26). The Gospel means more than that the dying Jesus is providing for His Mother's care. St. John's thought goes beyond such limited domestic details. The words of Jesus at the Last Supper serve as guide to the meaning of His words on Calvary. The night before He suffered He had said, "When a woman is in labor she is sad that her time has come. When she has borne her child, she no longer remembers her pain for joy that a man has been born into the world" (Jn 16:21). The

Old Testament promised that in the messianic age the Daughter of Zion would bring forth children she had never conceived. Israel's longing for the Messiah was sometimes compared to the pains of labor. The words "Woman, there is your son; there is your mother" contain the solemn announcement that the messianic promise has come true. Mary on Calvary symbolizes the "woman" who is mother Church, the new Israel, the new People of God, the mother of all men, Jew and Gentile. "The Mother of Jesus brings forth in him and with him that whole new people that is to spring from his resurrection; all these children Mary carries in her womb as she once carried Jesus." [8] "The importance of this action is emphasized by the words that follow: 'After this, Jesus, knowing that all was now accomplished. . . .' It is the climax of Jesus' deeds on the cross, the climax of his 'hour,' because it sets the Church on its path, creating the community of love between those he loves." [9]

Chapter Two
THE CHURCH'S UNDERSTANDING OF THE MYSTERY OF MARY

38 The understanding of Mary in Christian history unfolded along the lines of the Scriptures. The Church saw herself symbolized in the Virgin Mary. The story of Mary, as the Church has come to see her, is at the same time the record of the Church's own self-discovery. The Second Vatican Council quoted St. Ambrose (d. 397): "The Mother of God is a model of the Church in the matter of faith, charity and perfect union with Christ." [10] "As the Church's model and excellent exemplar in faith and charity," [11] Mary stands out as uniquely virgin and mother within the Church, itself rightly called virgin and mother.[12] As the Virgin Mary conceived and brought forth Jesus, so the Church, virgin in purity of faith, brings forth His brethren at the baptismal font.

39 The Church appears in the New Testament as the "spotless bride of Christ," as "virgin," and as "mother." Christians early learned to speak of "mother Church." Mary's virginal conception of Jesus, and her life-long virginal vocation, were taken as the model of the Church's virginal faith. The Church keeps faith with Christ the Bridegroom, who will make His bride spotless, free from every stain.

The New Eve

40 After the Scriptures, the oldest consideration of the Virgin Mary by Christian writers is that she is the "new Eve." St. Justin (d. 165) contrasts Mary with the first Eve, and St. Irenaeus (d. ca. 202) develops this much further. In writing of the recapitulation of all things in Christ, the new Adam, Irenaeus says:

> "If the former, Eve, did disobey God, yet the latter, Mary, was persuaded to be obedient to God in order that the Virgin Mary might become the advocate of the virgin

Eve. And thus, as the human race fell into bondage to death by means of a virgin, so it is rescued by a virgin, a virgin's disobedience having been balanced in the scale by virginal obedience." [13]

41 The early comparisons were between the disobedient Eve and the obedient new Eve. Eve believed the word of deceit; the new Eve heeded Gabriel's message. A woman helped introduce death; Mary became "the cause of salvation" and "advocate of Eve." By St. Jerome's time (d. 420) it was common to hear: "death through Eve, life through Mary." [14] Even more anciently, the Church was regarded as the "new Eve." The Church is the bride of Christ, formed from His side in the sleep of death on the cross, as the first Eve was formed by God from the side of the sleeping Adam. As the first Eve was "mother of the living," the Church becomes the "new mother of the living." In time, some of the maternal characteristics of the Church were seen in Mary, and so St. Epiphanius (d. 403) calls Mary "the mother of the living." [15]

The Virginal Conception

42 We commented briefly above on the virginal conception and birth of Jesus. Here it may be helpful to speak further on this doctrine. Both St. Luke and St. Matthew bear witness to the fact that Jesus had no human father. St. Luke brings this out in relating Mary's question (1:34) and St. Matthew in telling of Joseph's dream (1:20-25). Some of the Fathers read an allusion to the Virgin birth in St. John's reference to those "begotten not by blood, nor by carnal desire, nor by man's willing it, but by God" (1:13).

43 The Gospel of Mark has no infancy chapters and is silent about the Virgin birth, as is the rest of the New Testament. What is normative in the matter of the Virgin birth is the teaching of the Church. The Bible is read rightly in the Church, whose interpretation is guided by the Holy Spirit. This guidance of the Holy Spirit is experienced at many levels within the Church: 1) in the "sense of the faithful," i.e., the unerring instinct for truth of the Christian people; 2) in the faithful and loving work of Christian theologians; 3) in a very important way in the liturgy and approved prayers of all Christians; 4) and especially in the magisterial teaching of popes and bishops, whether expressed solemnly in ecumenical councils and *ex cathedra* definitions of the pope or through ordinary teaching channels.

44 In the creed we profess that Jesus was "born of the Virgin Mary." Our Catholic profession of faith in the Virgin birth is not based on a theoretical acceptance of the possibility of virgin births, which is then applied to the particular fact of the human origin of Jesus. We affirm that "we believe in Jesus Christ, his only Son our Lord, who was conceived by the Holy Spirit and born of the Virgin Mary. . . ." The creedal phrases go together to confess the unique mystery of Jesus the Savior, Son of God, Son of Mary, bound up with the mystery "that we might receive the adoption of sons." The Virgin birth is not merely a symbolical way of describing God's intervention in human history, not just a literary device to convey the divine preexistence of the Word. Nor is the Virgin birth a human construct, as if Christians feared that the divinity of Jesus would be compromised by His having a human father. What really matters here is the manner in which God in fact chose to "send his Son in the fullness of time." We know what God has done, not only from the text of Bible, taken in isolation, but from the Bible as read, interpreted, and understood by the living Church, guided by the Holy Spirit. Catholic belief in the Virgin birth rests not on the Scriptures alone, but on the constant and consistent faith of the Church. Faith on this precise point has been expressed in many ways from the time of St. Matthew and St. Luke to the present.

45 Many of our beliefs have been taught by the Church without ever having been solemnly defined either by ecumenical councils or by popes invoking their supreme teaching authority. In addition to crisis situations and special needs, the Church has its normal gradual growth in belief and practice. Early Christian writers and creeds repeated the phrase, "born of the Virgin Mary." By the second century, elements of the Apostles' Creed make their appearance in various documents. Ignatius of Antioch (d. ca. 110) wrote to the Christians of Smyrna of "the Son of God . . . truly born of a virgin." St. Justin in the middle of the second century sees the Isaian prophecy (Is 7:14) fulfilled in the Virgin birth, and calls the Mother of Jesus simply "Virgin Mary." St. Irenaeus looks more deeply into the mystery: "Because an unexpected salvation was to be initiated for men through God's help, an unexpected birth from a Virgin was likewise accomplished. The sign was God-given; the effect was not manmade."[16] Irenaeus' disciple, Hippolytus, records this third-century creed: "I believe in God, the Father Almighty, and in Christ Jesus, Son of God, who was born from the Holy Spirit of Mary the Virgin."[17]

46 In the understanding of the Church, as well as of Sts. Matthew and Luke, the virginal conception is not accomplished at the expense of the full humanity of Jesus, always insisted upon by Christian faith. If miracles be rejected out of hand, then the Virgin birth will be ruled out as antecedently impossible. Catholic faith, however, does not see God as "a prisoner of his own eternity."[18] In the Virgin birth He has intervened in a truly unique way. The loving graciousness of God has offered mankind a fresh beginning in Christ, the new Adam. The conception of Jesus is not due to procreation through human love, exalted though this may be, but to the Spirit of divine love.

47 The Old Testament tells of many marvelous births in preparation for the Messiah, of children sent to elderly couples, as were Isaac, son of Abraham and Sarah, and Samuel, son of Hannah. In the gospels, there is John the Baptist, son of Zachary and Elizabeth, immediate forerunner of Christ. These unexpected births were signs that salvation comes from God.

48 The virginal conception of Jesus is the climax and goal of this great series, totally surpassing human hopes and human means. The same God who sanctifies human sexuality and procreation, God the Creator, who made the marriage law of "two in one flesh . . . increase and multiply," has at the dawn of the new creation shown His independence of normal ways. It was prophesied in the Old Testament that the Spirit would revivify all things, would create a new people, renew the face of the earth. The overshadowing Spirit who brings about the virginal conception of the Son of Mary is the same powerful Spirit. The Virgin birth is not simply a privilege affecting only Jesus and Mary, but a sign and means for the Spirit to build the new People of God, the Body of Christ, the Church. The glorious positive sign value of the Virgin birth is the merciful and free saving grace of the Father sending His Son, conceived by the Holy Spirit, born of the Virgin Mary, that we might receive the adoption of Sons.

Always A Virgin

49 The truth that Mary remained always a virgin, that is, that she had no other children and never used her marital rights, emerges clearly in the Church's consciousness in the 4th century, when "ever-virgin" became a common description of her. This truth was accepted by all Christians until the Reformation. Groups of Christian ascetics were able to form after the peace of Constantine in the early 4th century. Consecrated virgins and celibate monks and hermits gave their lives to the keeping of the evangelical counsels, witnessing to Christ by lives of poverty, obedience and voluntary virginity. In prayerful reflection and in their own experience of this type of dedication, these Christians discovered in Mary an exemplar of virginal consecration to Christ. This experience, freely chosen by some and held in general honor by the Christian people, provided insights into the mystery of Mary ever-virgin that the Church recognized as guided by the Holy Spirit. In the writings of St. Athanasius of Alexandria (d. 373), of St. Ambrose (d. 397), of St. Augustine (d. 430), and of St. Jerome (d. 420), our Lady's lifelong virginity is praised. St. Jerome faced the difficulties in such Biblical expressions as "brothers of the Lord." He showed that in New Testament Greek this term can mean "cousins" as well as "blood brothers."[19] By the time of the Council of Ephesus, 431 A.D., belief in the perpetual virginity of Mary was well formulated.

50 This teaching about Mary's lifelong virginity is an example of the Church's growth in understanding of Christian doctrine. In its ordinary teaching, reflected in catechesis and liturgy, as well as in more formal pronouncements, the Church has here recognized as an aspect of "public revelation" a belief not clearly demonstrable from the Scriptures. In Mary's virginal dedication to her Son's saving work, the Church sees delineated her own mission to bear witness to values that go beyond the secular city to the city of redeemed man, the kingdom of God, in its present reality as well as in its future completion. The Dogmatic Constitution on the Church repeated this conviction, urging religious to "pattern (themselves) after that manner of virginal and humble life which Christ the Lord elected for himself and which His Virgin Mother also chose."[20]

The Blessedness of Mary

51 In the Bible "blessed" is the preferred description of the Mother of Jesus. Considering how infrequently the Gospel writers praise individuals, the insistence on Mary's blessedness is evidence of the veneration in which the early Church held her. John Macquarrie, Anglican theologian, suggests that the beatitudes help us understand how the word "blessed" is particularly associated with Mary: "The qualities set forth there are those which we see also in the Blessed Virgin. So the blessedness of the Virgin adumbrates the blessedness of the Church—no earthly happiness, but a 'likeness to God,' which means a participation in God's self-giving love. . . ." [21] The gospel of St. Luke witnesses to the belief of the primitive Church in Mary's unique holiness: "All ages to come will call me blessed. . . . God who is mighty has done great things for me" (Lk 1:48). In her, above all others, was realized the promise of our Lord "blest are those who hear the word of God and keep it" (Lk 11:28).

52 The Virgin Mary was called by the Fathers of the Church "all holy," the term beloved to this day by Christians in the East. She was declared to be "free from all stain of sin," "fashioned by the Holy Spirit into a kind of new substance and a new creature." The Second Vatican Council asserts that she was "adorned with the radiance of a singular holiness from the first moment of her conception. . . ." [22] In this statement, the Council calls attention to the doctrine of the Immaculate Conception. In 1854 Pope Pius IX defined as revealed truth "that the Blessed Virgin Mary in the first instant of her conception, by a singular grace and privilege of almighty God, in view of the foreseen merits of Jesus Christ the Savior of the human race, was preserved free from all stain of original sin." [23]

53 Conceived and born of human parents in the normal way, Mary was especially gifted by God from "the first instant of her conception." The grace which others receive in Baptism, God gave to Mary even before her birth, through the foreseen merits of Christ, to prepare her to be the Mother of the Redeemer. The doctrine of the Immaculate Conception is doubly Christ-centered. It makes clear, first of all, that no one is saved apart from Christ. This is true of all men who have ever lived, even though they were born many centuries before Christ. Secondly, the preservative redemption of Mary is totally and splendidly God's gift to her because she was to be the Mother of Christ.

54 In one of his first sermons after he became a Catholic, John Henry Newman asserted the great principle contained in our Lord's words, "More blessed is it to do God's will than to be God's Mother." He wrote: "Never say . . . that Catholics forget this passage of Scripture. Whenever they keep the feast of the Immaculate Conception, the Purity, or the like, recollect it is because they make so much of the blessedness of sanctity. . . . For the honor of the Son she (the Church) has ever extolled the glory of the Mother." [24]

55 As the Council put it, "By thus consenting to the divine utterance, Mary, a daughter of Adam, became the Mother of Jesus. Embracing God's saving will with a full heart and impeded by no sin, she devoted herself totally as a handmaid of the Lord to the person and work of her Son. In subordination to Him and along with Him, by the grace of almightly God she served the mystery of redemption." [25] "The Blessed Virgin was eternally predestined, in conjunction with the Incarnation of the divine Word to be the Mother of God" (n. 61, repeating a phrase from Pope Pius IX). For "the Father of Mercies willed that the consent of the predestined mother should precede the Incarnation. . . ." [26] The Mother of the Lord was early regarded by popular piety as singularly holy even in her origin, and a feast of the "conception of holy Mary" was celebrated in some countries as early as the 8th or 9th centuries.[27]

56 Mary's initial holiness, a totally unmerited gift of God, is a sign of the love of Christ for His Bride the Church, which, though composed of sinners, is still "holy Church." Mary Immaculate is seen in relation to Christ and the Church. Her privileged origin is the final step in preparing mankind to receive the Redeemer. God's grace triumphed over the power of original sin; the Father chose a perfectly responsive mother for the incarnate Son. The grace of the Immaculate Conception, a charism totally from God, prepared Mary for the motherhood of Jesus, the Savior. The Virgin Mary is "the most excellent fruit of the redemption," [28] a figure of the spotless bride of Christ, which is the Church.

The Assumption

57 Another aspect of Our Lady's holiness is brought out in her oldest liturgical feast, the Assumption. The meaning of this doctrine is that Mary is one with the risen Christ in the fullness of her personality, or as we commonly say, "in body and soul." Pope Pius XII solemnly proclaimed on November 1, 1950: "The Immaculate Mother of God, Mary ever-virgin, after her life on earth, was assumed, body and soul, into heavenly glory." [29]

58 As early as the fifth century, Christians celebrated a "Memorial of Mary," patterned on the "birthday into heaven" of the martyrs' anniversaries. By this they gave prayer form to their belief in the resurrection of the body and in the special bond between holy Mary and Jesus, the risen Savior. This primitive "Memorial of Mary," sometimes observed on August 15, evolved into the feast of the Dormition (the "falling asleep") of the Virgin. As early as the 6th century, homilies on the Assumption appear,[30] which bring out the abiding and perfect conformity of the Mother of Jesus with "her Son, the Lord of lords, and the Conqueror of sin and death." [31] An 8th century prayer, originally an announcement of a procession on August 15, has survived as an entrance prayer in some Western liturgies (e.g., the Carmelite rite until recently): "On this day the holy Mother of God suffered temporal death, but could not be held fast by the bonds of death, who gave birth to our Lord made flesh."

59 United to the victorious Christ in heaven, Mary is "the image and first-flowering of the Church as she is to be perfected in the world to come." She shines forth "as a sign of sure hope and solace for the pilgrim People of God." [32] In her Assumption, Mary manifests the fullness of redemption, and appears as the "spotless image" of the Church responding in joy to the invitation of the Bridegroom Christ, himself the "first fruits of those who have fallen asleep" (1 Cor 15:20).

60 Christ has risen from the dead; we need no further assurance of our faith. "Mary assumed into heaven" serves rather as a gracious reminder to the Church that our Lord wishes all whom the Father has given him to be raised with him. In Mary taken to glory, to union with Christ, the Church sees herself answering the invitation of the heavenly Bridegroom.

61 There is a tender note here that is at the same time profoundly doctrinal, for it is based on the real humanity of the risen Jesus. Archbishop Philip Pocock of Toronto expresses it this way: "Jesus does not wish to be alone, but face-to-face with another in love. Our Lady sharing in the glory of her Son strengthens our hope in the destiny of the entire Church. This was the vision of St. John, when, contemplating the age to come, he saw the holy city, the new Jerusalem, coming down out of heaven from God, made ready as a bride adorned for her husband" (Rv 21:2).[33] The Mother of Jesus stands facing the risen Savior, her Son, a joyful sign to the Church of the answer to its constant prayer, "Come, Lord Jesus." The documents of the Second Vatican Council use several Biblical images for the Church. It is called not only the "body," favored by St. Paul, consisting of Christ as Head and Christians as members, but also "People of God," and "bride." In a good marriage, their very union perfects the partners as individuals. Similarly, the mystical marriage between Christ and His Church perfects the bride (and hence each member of the Church) in and through union with the Bridegroom. Mary in her Assumption, as in other aspects of her God-gifted personality, is a figure of the Church as perfected through union with Christ.

Mother of God

62 In the liturgy "we honor Mary the ever-virgin Mother of Jesus Christ our Lord and God" (Eucharistic Prayer I); "Mary, the virgin Mother of God" (Prayers II and III); and "the Virgin Mary, the Mother of God" (Prayer IV). Cardinal Newman's phrase, "The Glories of Mary for the Sake of Her Son,"[34] is supremely applicable to the title "Mother of God," which was declared to be the faith of the Church at the Third Ecumenical Council, held at Ephesus, in 431 A.D. The Church's insistence on this title, Mother of God, is understandable, since no other formula makes so evident the intimate link between devotion to the Virgin Mary and belief in the Incarnation. This title was already in use in parts of the Church as early as the third century. The original form of the familiar prayer, "We fly to thy patronage, O holy Mother of God" may also be that early.

63 The term "Mother of God" was used in Christian prayers before the doctrinal controversy that made it a test phrase of

Christian faith. In 428 A.D. the term "Mother of God" was publicly challenged in Constantinople. The Church reacted strongly to this challenge at the Council of Ephesus. At stake was the central Christian truth that the man Jesus, Son of Mary, is truly "Son of God." Mary can be rightly called "Mother of God," not indeed in the blasphemous sense of having existed before God, but as an affirmation of the truth of the Incarnation. The Son of Mary is the one person who is the Son of God, Emmanuel.

64   St. Cyril of Alexandria spoke for the Church's traditional faith when he wrote: "If we are to confess that Emmanuel is truly God, we must also confess that the Holy Virgin is *Theotokos* (Mother of God); for she bore according to the flesh the Word of God made flesh." St. Cyril's explanation of the term "Mother of God" shows that the center of attention must be Christ himself: "Nor was he first born of the holy Virgin as an ordinary man, in such a way that the Word only afterwards descended upon him; rather was he united with flesh in the womb itself, and thus is said to have undergone birth according to the flesh, inasmuch as he makes his own the birth of his own flesh. . . . For this reason the holy Fathers have boldly proclaimed the holy Virgin *Theotokos*."[35] Subsequent ecumenical councils, such as Chalcedon, 451 A.D., and II Constantinople, 553 A.D., made the meaning of "Mother of God" even more precise.

Chapter Three
MARY, MEDIATRIX AND SPIRITUAL MOTHER

65 "Mediatrix" is a familiar Catholic term to describe the unique role of the Mother of Jesus in her Son's mission as Mediator. We need to consider the meaning of "mediatrix," since some have the erroneous impression that the Second Vatican Council minimized or even denied the mediation of Mary. Although it used the word, mediatrix, only once, and altogether avoided the words "co-redemptrix" and "dispensatrix," the Council both retained and deepened Catholic understanding of our Lady's mediatorial role.

66 For the Council's restricted use of the word "mediatrix" there was a double reason: one ecumenical, the other pastoral. Ecumenically, "mediatrix" has seemed to many who are not Catholics to clash with the Biblical insistence on Jesus Christ as our one Mediator (1 Tm 2:5). Pastorally, the bishops were anxious that Catholics understand even better Mary's true place under Christ. As mediatrix, Mary takes away nothing from Christ's all-sufficient mediatorship. It is owing to the Redeemer that all the redeemed are enabled to share in the Savior's work, and to influence the salvation of their brothers and sisters in the body of Christ. Through her life of faith on earth, and now through her union with the risen Christ, the Mother of Jesus is the supreme example of loving association with the Savior in His mission of redeeming mankind. The manner in which men share in the Savior's redeeming work is similar to the way Christians, both ordained ministers and other believers, share in the priesthood of Christ, and, indeed, to the way all creatures share in the undivided goodness of the Creator."[36]

67 Pope Paul put it this way: "Since Mary is rightly to be regarded as the way by which we are led to Christ, the person who encounters Mary cannot help but encounter Christ likewise."[37] Father Frederick Jelly explains how Mary's mediation, far from being a new role, fosters "immediate union of the faithful with Christ."[38] Father Jelly writes: "Mary is not a bridge over the gap that separates us from a remote Christ. . . . Such an approach to Marian devotion and doctrine would minimize the deepest meaning of the Incarnation, the fact that he has become a man like us, and that his sacred humanity has made him the unique mediator between God and us. Mary's greatness is that she brought him close to us, and her mediation continues to create the spiritual climate for our immediate encounter with Christ."[39]

68 St. Paul saw himself as the herald of Christ Jesus, the one Mediator. Nevertheless in the same letter to Timothy in which he extols the unique mediatorship of Christ, the apostle calls upon all to share in God's saving plan by offering prayers, petitions, intercessions and thanksgivings (1 Tm 2:1). What St. Paul urges is in fact a sharing in the mission of Christ the Mediator. Mary's mediatorial role, correctly understood, is in perfect accord with the centrality of Christ.

69 What is the positive value of Mary's role as mediatrix, and how does she exercise it? The Gospels portray her as a woman who walked by faith from the time of the Annunciation to Pentecost. The Virgin of Nazareth belonged to a family circle that was awaiting the consolation of Israel (Lk 2:5). The Mother of Jesus appears as totally responsive to the Father's will, always one with her Son's purposes, led by the Holy Spirit in everything.[40] "Be it done unto me according to your word" (Lk 1:38) was the act of faith of the Lord's handmaid, a sign of her unwavering service to God in every detail of her life. In the Scriptures, "faith" means surrender of heart and body as well as of mind and intellect. St. Luke writes of Mary "reflecting in her heart" (Lk 2:19, 51). St. John records the advice she exemplified in her own life: "Do whatever he tells you" (Jn 2:5). The Gospels provide few details of Mary's life; but they do delineate a remarkable portrait of the woman who gave herself wholeheartedly to her Son and His mission in perfect faith, love and obedience. What Mary began on earth in association with the saving mission of Jesus, she continues still, in union with the risen Christ.

Spiritual Mother

70 It is a cherished American Catholic custom to call the Mother of Jesus "our Blessed Mother." In many respects this title can be explained in the same way as "mediatrix." Still, it has its own special value. "Mother" belongs to the language of the transmission of life. The reference here is to our life in Christ. St. Paul's familiar comparison likens the Church to a human body, with Christ as Head, and the faithful as its members. Like the Savior's parable of the vine and branches, the image of the Church as "body of Christ" is a graphic reminder that the same life links members to Head, branches to Vine. From earliest Christian times the Church was regarded as "Mother Church." Gradually, Mary's relationship to the sons and daughters of the Church came to be regarded also as that of "spiritual mother." Physically mother of Christ the Head, Mary is spiritually mother of the members of Christ. She is mother of all men, for Christ died for all. She is especially the mother of the faithful, or as Pope Paul proclaimed during the Second Vatican Council, she is "Mother of the Church."

71 It is important to understand what is meant by the title, "our Blessed Mother." Mary is not spiritual mother of men solely because she was physical Mother of the Savior. Nonetheless, the full understanding of Mary's motherhood of Jesus contains also the secret of her spiritual motherhood of the brethren of Christ. This secret is the truth already given in the Gospels and constantly stressed ever since in Christian thought and piety: Mary consented *in faith* to become the Mother of Jesus. The Second Vatican Council was in the stream of the constant tradition of the Church when it said that Mary received the Word of God into her heart and her body at the angel's announcement and thereby brought Life to the world.[41] She conceived in her heart, with her whole being, before she conceived in her womb. First came Mary's faith, then her motherhood. Faith is the key also to the spiritual motherhood of Mary. By her faith she became the perfect example of what the Gospels mean by "spiritual motherhood." In the preaching of the Savior, His "mother" is whoever hears God's word and keeps it. All who truly follow Christ become "mothers" of Christ, for by their faith they bring Him to birth in others.

72 The Council fathers make use of a beautiful passage from St. Augustine, describing Mary as "Mother of the members of Christ . . . since she cooperated out of love so that there might be born in the Church the faithful, who are members of Christ their head."[42] These words were used by Pope Pius XII in his encyclical letter of May 15, 1956 on the Sacred Heart. The strength of St. Augustine's words becomes evident when it is realized that he was commenting on two incidents from the public life, the so-called "difficult sayings" of the Lord. The first incident is found in St. Luke. He is the only evangelist to record the praise of the enthusiastic woman from the crowd: "Blest is the womb that bore you and the breasts that nursed you," and the reply of Jesus: "Rather, blest are they who hear the word of God and keep it" (Lk 11:28). The "true kinsmen" incident is told by Matthew (12:46-50) and Mark (3:31-35), as well as by Luke, who writes (8:19-21): "He was told, 'Your mother and your brothers are standing outside and they wish to see you.' He said in reply, 'My mother and my brothers are those who hear the word of God and act upon it.'"

73 The passage from St. Augustine quoted above comes from his treatise *On Christian Virginity* (about 401 A.D.). He writes: "More blessed was Mary in receiving the faith of Christ than in conceiving the flesh of Christ. For to her who said, 'Blessed is the womb that bore you and the breasts that nursed you,' he replied, 'Still more blessed are those who hear the word of God and keep it' (Lk 11:27-28). What in fact did their relationship profit his brethren according to the flesh who believed not in him? So too, even the close relationship of motherhood would have profited Mary nothing had she not also more blessedly borne Christ in her heart than in her flesh. . . ."

74 St. Augustine continues: "All holy virgins are, with Mary, mothers of Christ if they do his Father's will. For in this even Mary is with greater praise and blessedness Christ's Mother, according to the sentence, 'Whoever does the will of my Father who is in heaven, the same is my brother and sister and mother'" (Mt 12, 50). Commenting on this passage, Augustine explains: "All these relationships to himself he (Jesus) sets forth spiritually in the people whom he has redeemed. He has as brethren and sisters holy men and holy women, since they are co-heirs with him in the heavenly inheritance (Rom 8:17). The whole Church is his mother, because she it is who brings forth his members, that is, his faithful by the grace of God. His mother too is every good person who does his Father's will by means of charity, meaning a charity that is in labor for others until Christ be formed in them (Gal 4:15). And therefore Mary in doing God's will is mother of Christ in the flesh, but spiritually she is both sister and mother. . . . She is mother of the members of Christ, which we are, because through love she cooperated in the birth of the faithful in the Church, and they are members of that Head."

75 St. Augustine does not restrict spiritual motherhood to the Virgin Mary and to other virgins. For he writes a bit further on: "Both married women of the faith and virgins consecrated to God, by holy lives and by charity 'from a pure heart and a good conscience and faith unfeigned' (1 Tm 1:5) are spiritually the mothers of Christ because they do the will of his Father." [43]

76 The incidents from the public ministry used by St. Augustine occur frequently in the liturgy. St. Luke's narrative of the enthusiastic woman is often read at Marian Masses. Our Lord's reply intensifies the woman's simple praise: "Still more blessed those who hear the word of God and keep it." Elizabeth's words from the first chapter of St. Luke come to mind: "Blest are you among women and blest is the fruit of your womb. . . . Blest is she who trusted that the Lord's words to her would be fulfilled" (Lk 1:42, 45).

77 The other incident which refers to Mary is that of "the true kinsmen." St. Luke relates the event just after the parable of the Sower and the Seed in which Jesus likens the rich soil to persons who hear God's word "in a spirit of openness, retain it, and bear fruit through perseverance" (Lk 8:15). It is possible that St. Luke deliberately described the visit of the "mother and brothers" of Jesus just after the parable of the sower because of Mary. Mary is the person of noble and generous heart, the woman of faith who heard the word and took it to herself and yielded the great harvest through her perseverance, her love and her faith. Mary put into practice her Son's advice about the kingdom being above considerations of flesh and blood. Jesus proposed hearing the Word of God and keeping it as the norm of blessedness. His Mother kept the Word so faithfully that her life can be called a "pilgrimage of faith." St. Luke twice calls attention to Mary's "pondering in her heart": when the shepherds relate the experiences that brought them to Bethlehem (Lk 2:19); and in reaction to the mysterious word about "His Father's house" from her 12-year-old Son (Lk 2:51; cf. also Lk 1:29 and 2:33).

78 As a perfect disciple, the Virgin Mary heard the Word of God and kept it, to the lasting joy of the messianic generations who call her blessed. It is our Catholic conviction that in her present union with the risen Christ, our Blessed Mother is still solicitous for our welfare, still desirous that we become more like Jesus, her firstborn. The Mother of Jesus wishes all her other children, all men and all women, to reach the maturity of the fullness of Christ (Eph 4:13; Col 1:28).

79 Word of God—faith—birth of Christ: this is the pattern for the maternity of Mary and the maternity of the Church. Life is the dominant note in the language of motherhood. Mary brings forth Christ the Life; the Church continually regenerates men in the Christ-life. For both Mary and the Church, their motherhood is virginal, that is, entirely dependent on God, not on man. The Church's mission as "mother of the redeemed" was first realized in the Virgin Mother of Jesus. Open to the overshadowing Spirit, as was the Virgin Mary, the Church receives the Word of God and brings forth life. There are striking likenesses between the Annunciation and Pentecost. From the overshadowing of the Spirit, Christ is conceived; from the Pentecostal outpouring of the Spirit, Christ is born in His members who are the Church. Mary, the great mother figure for the Church, is present not only at the Annunciation, but praying with her Son's disciples before Pentecost.

80 Pondering the hidden holiness of Mary, the Church learns to imitate her charity and to carry out in faith the Father's will. Thereby the Church herself becomes a mother, receiving the Word of God in faith. By the ministry of the Word and Baptism, Mother Church brings forth to new life children conceived by the Holy Spirit and born of God. In imitation of the Mother of her Lord, by the power of His Spirit, the Church maintains an integral faith, a firm hope and a sincere charity.[44] In its apostolic work the Church looks to Mary. She conceived, brought forth, and nourished Christ.[45] So too, through the Church, Jesus continues to be born and grow in the hearts of the faithful.[46]

Chapter Four
MARY IN OUR LIFE

Mary's Intercession. Her Place in the Communion of Saints.

81 According to the *Constitution on the Sacred Liturgy,* the Church honors the Mother of God when it celebrates the cycle of Christ's saving mysteries. For "Blessed Mary is joined by an inseparable bond to the saving work of her Son." [47] Deeper Biblical insights have increased our awareness of Mary as the model of faithful discipleship; but it is also our purpose here to reinforce our Catholic sense of the Blessed Mother's present concern for us in her union with the risen Christ.

82 Since early times, but especially after the Council of Ephesus, devotion to Mary in the Church has grown wondrously. The People of God through the ages have shown her veneration and love. They have called upon her in prayer and they imitate her.[48] All these ways of praising Mary draw us closer to Christ. When Mary is honored, her Son is duly acknowledged, loved and glorified, and His commandments are observed.[49] To venerate Mary correctly means to acknowledge her Son, for she is the Mother of God. To love her means to love Jesus, for she is always the Mother of Jesus. To pray to our Lady means not to substitute her for Christ, but to glorify her Son who desires us to have loving confidence in His Saints, especially in His Mother. To imitate the "faithful Virgin" means to keep her Son's commandments.

83 The better we come to know Mary of the gospels as the Church views her in liturgical celebrations and popular commemorations, the more we will be led to imitate her. We may ask, however, how the two aspects of imitation and prayer are joined in devotion to Mary. Or, to put the question in another way: how are memory of the past and experiences of the present related in our devotion to the Mother of Jesus? Through the Bible we recall what Mary once was in her earthly association with

Jesus; but we also long to know what she means to us now, and why we pray to her. As Catholics, we believe that Mary was once joined to her Son's saving work on earth; but we also believe that she remains inseparably joined to Him, associated with the intercession the glorified Jesus makes for us forever at the throne of His Father (Heb 7:25).

84 All four Eucharistic Prayers contain a prayer of remembrance that names Mary. In Eucharistic Prayer III, after mentioning "Mary, the Virgin Mother of God, the apostles and martyrs and all your saints," we say that "on their constant intercession we rely for help." Intercession means that the blessed who are one with the risen Christ are still interested in us; they can and do pray for us. It is erroneous to think that the intercession of Mary and the saints is necessary in the sense that we do not have direct access to the merciful Savior. We believe that, having Christ, we have all things together with Him. However, it is part of God's loving plan that, even as we help one another on earth by our prayers and deeds, so we can rely on the blessed in heaven, above all the Blessed Virgin Mary, to assist us by their prayers.

85 There is little doubt that we are passing through a period marked by a lack of interest in the saints. Much more is involved here than devotion to the saints, even St. Mary. What is at stake is the reality of the humanity of the risen Jesus. There is danger of so spiritualizing the risen Christ that we diminish awareness of His humanity. It is our Christian belief that as man Jesus has taken His seat at the right hand of the Father; as man, Christ rose from the dead and ascended to heaven; as man, He lives forever to make intercession for us. When he was asked about the decline of Marian devotion, the German Jesuit, Father Karl Rahner, declared that the special temptation that affects Christians today, Catholics and Protestants alike, is the temptation to turn the central truths of the faith into abstractions, and abstractions have no need of mothers (quoted by Cardinal Suenens at Zagreb, August, 1971).[50]

86 The seventh chapter of the *Dogmatic Constitution on the Church*[51] concerns the relationship of the pilgrim Church to the Church in heaven, or, more familiarly, treats the "communion of saints." This strongly Scriptural chapter has been even more neglected than the chapter on our Blessed Lady. The Council reminds us of our Catholic belief that we are still united with our brothers and sisters who have fallen asleep in the peace of Christ. Far from being interrupted, our union with them is strengthened by a sharing of spiritual goods.

87   Father Herbert McCabe, O.P., explains: "Prayer for the dead is first of all an expression of our presence in Christ, not merely to our contemporaries, but to the men and women of the past. . . . Because Christ is risen and present to us we are more present to each other." In the risen Christ "we establish a deep and mysterious union with our fellow-men."[52] Christians live together in the Spirit of Christ; death cannot break this living community. Belief in the Resurrection does not mean that we think of Christ simply as a person from the past whom we still remember; belief in the risen Christ means that we are somehow in personal contact with Him, that the glorified Jesus is present to us.

88   For the same reason, Father McCabe adds, all "who have 'died in Christ' are also not merely objects of memory . . . in him they are really present to us and in him they will share the future we hope for." The Church has recognized that certain holy people, led by the Mother of the Lord, are already in glory. When we celebrate the memory of Mary in the liturgy, we join together in a present liturgical "moment" the past and the future—what Mary once was on earth, as the Gospels show her, and the future, our reunion with Mary and the saints, including the uncanonized saints of our own families, reunited in the risen Lord. The saints "have been received into their heavenly home and are present to the Lord. Through him, with him and in him, they do not cease to intercede with the Father for us."[53] Through their fraternal concern, our pilgrim weakness is greatly alleviated. We seek from the saints for our greater good and that of the Church "example in their way of life, fellowship in their communion, and aid by their intercession,"[54] as a new Preface says.[55]

89   The *Constitution on the Sacred Liturgy* states: "In the earthly liturgy, by way of foretaste we share in that heavenly liturgy which is celebrated in the holy city of Jerusalem toward which we journey as pilgrims, and in which Christ is sitting at the right hand of God. . . ."[56] Celebrating the Eucharistic sacrifice, we are most closely joined with the worship of the heavenly Church, as we unite to honor the memory first of all of "the ever-virgin Mother of Jesus Christ our Lord and God,"⁵⁷ of Mary who is the "image and first-flowering of the Church as she is to be perfected in the world to come."⁵⁸

90 In speaking of Catholic devotion to Mary, we must not neglect to mention the special honor paid to our Lady in the liturgy and theology of the Eastern rites. Some of the most beautiful and profound passages concerning the Mother of God were written by the Eastern Fathers of the Church. Even today, in almost every liturgical service, we find repeated use of three glorious titles for the Mother of the Lord: She is called "the all-holy one," "the one without even the slightest stain," and "the one blessed beyond all others."⁵⁹

Mary in Christian Devotion

91 What is the place of our Lady in Catholic prayer life? Many Catholics today are forgetful of the saints, and have little sense of being one with the blessed, when they celebrate the liturgy and in their other prayers and devotions. From an age of novenas to our Lady under many titles, and to certain favorite saints (one thinks readily of St. Anne, St. Francis Xavier, and St. Therese of Lisieux), we have passed abruptly to near silence about these friends of Christ. In spite of the urging of the *Constitution on the Sacred Liturgy* that we celebrate the feasts of our Lady and deepen the sense of her association in the central saving mysteries of Jesus the Savior, the Church is suffering a malaise with respect to the commemoration of Mary. Two numbers, 66-67, in the chapter on our Lady deal with the cult of Mary, and are filled with practical suggestions, e.g., let the liturgy provide the lead, even for non-liturgical devotions, which are encouraged, especially those which have enjoyed the Church's favor for a long time. A middle way is recommended between the extremes of too much and too little.⁶⁰

92 In writing this Pastoral Letter, our concern about our Lady is most keenly felt in the area of devotion. No survey is needed to show that all over the country many forms of Marian devotion have fallen into disuse, and others are taking an uncertain course. In an age avid for symbols (the peace medals and other signs of the young are evidence of this), the use of Catholic Marian symbols, such as the scapular and the Miraculous Medal, has noticeably diminished. Only a few years ago use of the rosary was a common mark of a Catholic, and it was customarily taught to children, both at home and in courses in religious instruction. Adults in every walk of life found strength in this familiar prayer which is biblically based and is filled with the thought of Jesus and His Mother in the "mysteries." The praying of the rosary has declined. Some Catholics feel that there has even been a campaign to strip the churches of statues of our Lady and the saints. Admittedly, many churches were in need of artistic reform; but one wonders at the severity of judgment that would find no place for a fitting image of the Mother of the Lord.

93 We view with great sympathy the distress our people feel over the loss of devotion to our Lady and we share their concern that the young be taught a deep and true love for the Mother of God. We Bishops of the United States wish to affirm with all our strength the lucid statements of the Second Vatican Council on the permanent importance of authentic devotion to the Blessed Virgin, not only in the liturgy, where the Church accords her a most special place under Jesus her Son, but also in the beloved devotions that have been repeatedly approved and encouraged by the Church and that are still filled with meaning for Catholics. As Pope Paul has reminded us, the rosary and the scapular are among these tested forms of devotion that bring us closer to Christ through the example and protection of His Holy Mother.

94 In this sensitive area, where it is not possible to assess and comment on all the individual aspects of concern or to enter into local differences of viewpoint, we offer to the faithful some suggestions to increase love and devotion to the Blessed Virgin. Above all, the renewed liturgy offers immense riches with respect to the Mother of the Lord. Having the liturgy in English increases these possibilities even more. Far from having minimized the place of our Lady, the present lectionary contains more readings than we had before, from Old Testament and New, arranged for our Lady's feasts and commemorations. In the current calendar, there are more optional days on which a Marian votive Mass may be celebrated, on Saturdays in particular. Pope Paul's missal of 1970 has many excellent new prayers for Mary's feasts, based on the Bible and in the spirit of the Council. Among the more than 80 prefaces of the Sacramentary there are four of our Lady: two for regular use, one for the Immaculate Conception, and another for the Assumption.

95 Our bond with the saints, and St. Mary at their head, has its noblest expression in the liturgy, where we praise with joy the majesty of God. "Celebrating the Eucharistic sacrifice, therefore, we are most closely united to the worshipping Church in heaven as we join with and venerate the memory first of all of the glorious ever-Virgin Mary, of blessed Joseph and the blessed apostles and martyrs and of all the saints." [61]

96 Besides her place in the liturgy, our Lady has been honored by an amazingly rich variety of extra-liturgical devotional forms. Some of these have a long history. In particular the Dominican rosary of 15 decades links our Lady to her Son's salvific career, from the Annunciation and the joyful events of the infancy and childhood of Jesus, through the sorrowful mysteries of His suffering and death, to His Resurrection and Ascension, and the sending of the Spirit to the apostles at Pentecost, and concluding with the Mother's reunion with her Son in the mysteries of Assumption and Coronation. It is unwise to reject the rosary without a trial simply because of the accusation that it comes from the past, that it is repetitious and ill-suited to sophisticated moderns. The Scriptural riches of the rosary are of permanent value. Its prayers, in addition to the opening Apostles' Creed and the occasional repetition of the ancient and simple doxology (Glory be to the Father), are the "Our Father" and the "Hail Mary." The words of the first half of the Hail Mary are taken from St. Luke. The second half: "Holy Mary, Mother of God, pray for us sinners, now and at the hour of our death," is in the mainstream of prayers that go back to the early centuries of Christian devotion.[62]

97 The recommended saying of the rosary does not consist merely in "telling the beads" by racing through a string of familiar prayers. Interwoven with the prayers are the "mysteries." Almost all of these relate saving events in the life of Jesus, episodes in which the Mother of Jesus shared. Nor is rhythmic prayer alien to modern man, as is shown by the attraction of Eastern religions for many young people today. Besides the precise rosary pattern long known to Catholics, we can freely experiment. New sets of mysteries are possible. We have customarily gone from the childhood of Jesus to His Passion, bypassing the whole public life. There is rich matter here for rosary meditation, such as the wedding feast of Cana, and incidents from the public life where Mary's presence and Mary's name serve as occasions for her Son to give us a lesson in discipleship: "Still more blessed are they who hear the word of God and keep it" (Lk 11:28). Rosary vigils have already been introduced in some places, with an instructive use of readings, from Old Testament as well as New, and with recitation of a decade or two, if not all five. In a public celebration of the rosary, hymns can be introduced as well, and time allowed for periods of silent prayer.

98 The rosary suggestions here sketched can be applied to other devotional practices as well. In these changing times great inventiveness on the part of the whole Catholic people is needed. Under the guidance of the Holy Father and the bishops we must revitalize old forms and devise new devotions corresponding to current needs and desires. The liturgical season should set the tone for Marian prayers at each particular time of the year, e.g., May devotions should reflect paschal and pentecostal orientations.[63] Advent provides a unique opportunity for the consideration of Mary, in whom all Old Testament hopes culminated. Following her example, the Church awaits the Lord, not only in His coming at Bethlehem, but also in His second coming, and indeed in that daily presence to which the Church as bride must ever be sensitive.

99 We turn our reflections now to the authenticated appearances of our Lady and their influence on Catholic devotion especially in the years since the Apparition at Lourdes, in 1858. Other 19th century events of this kind were the experiences of St. Catherine Laboure in 1830 (the "Miraculous Medal"), and the apparition at La Salette in 1846. In our own hemisphere we recall the apparition in 1531 of Our Lady of Guadalupe, "Queen of the Americas." Best known of the 20th century appearances of the Mother of the Lord is that at Fatima, in 1917.

100 These providential happenings serve as reminders to us of basic Christian themes: prayer, penance, and the necessity of the sacraments. After due investigation, the Church has approved the pilgrimages and other devotions associated with certain private revelations. She has also at times certified the holiness of their recipients by beatification and canonization, for example, St. Bernadette of Lourdes and St. Catherine Laboure. The Church judges the devotions that have sprung from these extraordinary events in terms of its own traditional standards. Catholics are encouraged to practice such devotions when they are in conformity with authentic devotion to Mary. Even when a "private revelation" has spread to the entire world, as in the case of Our Lady of Lourdes, and has been recognized in the liturgical calendar, the Church does not make mandatory the acceptance either of the original story or of particular forms of piety springing from it. With the Vatican Council we remind true lovers of our Lady of the danger of superficial sentiment and vain credulity.[64] Our faith does not seek new gospels, but leads us to know the excellence of the Mother of God and moves us to a filial love toward our Mother and to the imitation of her virtues.[65]

The Blessed Virgin and Ecumenism

101 We live in a new era of friendly relations between Catholics and members of other Christian Churches, Orthodox, Anglican and Protestant. Often in the past, even fairly recently, the matter of Mary caused acrimonious differences between Catholics and Protestants. The dialogues of recent years, thanks to initiatives taken on both sides (on the Catholic side especially through the Second Vatican Council), have brought Christians to consider the difficulties of doctrine about and devotion to Mary openly and with charity. It would be naive to suggest that openness and mutual love can suddenly break down barriers erected on both sides over centuries. Yet encouraging signs appear. Catholics have been spurred on by the Second Vatican Council to "return to the Bible" for a profounder understanding of the Mother of Jesus as woman of faith. Brother Max Thurian of the French Calvinist monastery of Taize has put all Christians in his debt with a valuable book on the Mary of the Gospels: *Mary, Mother of the Lord, Figure of the Church.*[66]

102 Taking their cue from the Council's careful language, and profiting from its advice to "painstakingly guard against any word or deed which could lead separated brethren or anyone else into error regarding the true doctrine of the Church"[67] about our Lady, Catholic theology and piety of the last few years have been more discriminating in the use of such words as "mediatrix."

This term, as we mentioned before, was used only once by the fathers of Vatican II. Of ecumenical import also are Catholic efforts to show that such beliefs about the Mother of the Lord as her initial freedom from original sin (the Immaculate Conception) and her final union with the risen Christ (the Assumption) are not isolated privileges, but mysteries filled with meaning for the whole Church.

103 For too long Mary's place in Catholic doctrine and, even more, in Catholic devotion has been a sharp point of difference with other Christians of the West. What began in the Reformation as a reaction against certain abuses, soon led in some quarters to forbidding all invocation of the saints, even of Saint Mary, and to a diminished sense of the communion of saints. Throughout the Reformation and Counter-Reformation, excesses abounded on both sides. Protestant polemicists made a battle cry of the supposedly fatal choices: Christ or Mary, Scripture or Tradition, grace or freedom, God or man, as if Catholics did not also accept Christ and the Bible and the supremacy of grace and God as central to the faith.

104 The Catholic counterattack exalted and extolled Mary as "conqueror of all heresy." It seemed to many Protestants that the Roman Catholic Church had moved even farther away from Christ the Center, when Pius IX defined the Immaculate Conception of Mary in 1854, and Pius XII her Assumption in 1950. Karl Barth was fully in the Reformed tradition in his strong rejection of what he called "the Mariological dogma." He saw this as the sign *par excellence* of the Roman Church, which was to him "that church of man who, prompted by the grace of God, cooperates with grace and merits salvation." [68]

105 The role of the Mother of Jesus remains one of our many persisting religious differences, even though we are now better able to speak openly and charitably, putting aside old prejudices in common efforts to seek out what we share jointly in our Christian heritage and also where and why we differ.

106 We are convinced that all Christians share a basic reverence for the Mother of Jesus, a veneration deeper than doctrinal differences and theological disputes. We share a common past. Together we accept the Gospel respect for the Mother of Jesus, handmaid of the Lord, woman of faith, model of prayer, servant of the Spirit. The faith of the Church is anchored in history and, Mary is part of that anchor. Mentioned with Pontius Pilate in the Creed (but for a greatly different reason!), she attests to the historicity of Jesus Christ. In the early Church and in the first ecumenical councils, attention was focused on Jesus Christ, truly man and truly God. The phrase, "born of the Virgin Mary," was used in the second century to defend the reality of Jesus' humanity. At Ephesus, in 431 A.D., the divine motherhood was defined in defense of the divinity of the Son of Mary. The title, "Mother of God" became a permanent part of the creeds and liturgies of the entire Church. We have seen above how the Church recognized many aspects of herself in the Mother of Jesus —as virgin, as mother, as holy. The Middle Ages explored still further the likenesses between Mary and the Church. The emphasis on the heavenly intercession of the Mother of God strengthened the sense of community between the pilgrim Church on earth and the Church triumphant in heaven. With St. Luke as a basis, earlier times had made much of the Annunciation. The Middle Ages pondered Mary's compassion on Calvary, leading to the familiar representations of the Pieta.

107 We ask our brothers in other Christian Churches to re-examine with us Mary's place in our common patrimony. To an encouraging degree this is already being done in Bible studies and in the return to the study of the Fathers. The generally favorable reaction outside the Catholic Church to the Council's document on the Blessed Virgin Mary is encouraging indeed. Our Christian brothers have shown sensitivity to the conciliar use of Scripture and of the early Christian authors. They have also expressed appreciation of the restraint exercised by the Council with regard to the difficult term, "mediatrix." Perhaps most encouraging of all, they have paid notice to the reference in the *Decree on Ecumenism* to "the hierarchy of truths," which "vary in their relationship to the foundation of the Christian faith." [69]

108 The document on ecumenism brings out this "hierarchy of truths" with regard to the differences that still divide Western Christians, in spite of our common formula of Trinitarian and Christological faith. "Our thoughts are concerned first of all with those Christians who openly confess Jesus Christ as God and Lord and as the sole Mediator between God and man, unto the glory of the one God, Father, Son and the Holy Spirit. We are indeed aware that among them views are held considerably different from the doctrine of the Catholic Church even concerning Christ, God's Word made flesh, and the work of redemption, and thus concerning the mystery and ministry of the Church, and the role of Mary in the work of salvation." [70]

109 No sound ecumenism can ignore the question of Mary. "Marian truths cannot be pushed to one side, because there are no such things as isolated Christian truths which concern Mary alone." [71] She no more stands alone without Christ now than she did in the Scriptures or at Ephesus or in the liturgy, as it has been celebrated through the ages in the Eastern and Western rites. Christ is at the center of our faith; but He did not come among men without the *Theotokos*. Nor is He in glory now without His Mother, *Theotokos* still.

110 Another difficulty among Christians is the relationship between Scripture, Tradition and the Church's teaching role. How have Catholics come to regard as revealed truth such doctrines as Mary's Immaculate Conception and Assumption, in the absence of clear Biblical evidence? And, most difficult of all, is the problem: what can man do under the power of grace? The chief reason why "silence about Mary" is an ecumenically destructive policy is that one's attitude toward the mystery of Mary shows his position on this important question.[72]

111 What the Church has said about the effects of redemption in Mary, she has affirmed in other ways and at other times of us all. The Immaculate Conception and the Assumption, as we sought to show earlier in this letter, are basically affirmations about the nature of human salvation. "Mary is today, even as at Ephesus, a witness to the Incarnation. She was then a pointer to the truly historical reality of Jesus Christ who is God. Today she must be seen as indicating the full implications of the Incarnation for our understanding of being human." [73]

112 Another matter we might profitably explore together as Christians is the bond between Mary and the Holy Spirit. Christ sent His Spirit as the new Advocate, as the Intercessor who comes to help us in our weakness. Any correct understanding of Mary's role must be seen in connection with the predominant role of the

Holy Spirit. The Bible provides us with a starting point: St. Luke presents Mary as the humble woman overshadowed by the Holy Spirit in order that Christ be formed. "God sent his Son born of a woman . . . that we might receive the adoption of sons" (Gal 4:4).[74]

Chapter Five
MARY, MOTHER OF THE CHURCH

113 The title, "Mother of the Church," was announced by Pope Paul VI during the Council. The proclamation came after the promulgation of the *Dogmatic Constitution on the Church,* November 21, 1964. The Pope chose the occasion to give Mary a title "that expresses with wonderful brevity the exalted place in the Church which the Church recognizes as proper to the Mother of God." [75] The Holy Father desired to state in a single phrase the spiritual motherhood that the Mother of Jesus exercises toward the members of the "Mystical Body," the Church, of which Christ is Head. The Council set out to show forth the true beauty of the face of the Church, Spouse of Christ, and our teacher and mother. What the Council said about Mary's role in the mystery of Christ and His Church harmonized perfectly with this aim, and Pope Paul hoped that the title, "Mother of the Church" would call attention to the Council's teaching.

114 In this title, the "Church," of which Mary is Mother, is seen as comprising both shepherds and flocks, both pastors and people. As a believing disciple of Jesus, Mary can be called *daughter* of the Church, and our *sister* as well. For, like us, she has been redeemed by Christ, although in an eminent and privileged way.[76] What is the special significance of the title "Mother of the Church"? It is based on Mary's being the Mother of God. By God's call and her free response in the power of His grace, Mary became the Mother of Jesus, Son of God made man, and thus truly "Mother of God."

115 She remained joined to her Son's saving work in the new economy in which He freed men from sin by the mysteries of His flesh.[77] On Calvary, Jesus gave John into Mary's care and thus designated her Mother of the human race which the beloved disciple represented. At the Annunciation, Mary conceived Christ by the power of the Holy Spirit. After Christ's Resurrection, surrounded by His disciples, Mary prayed for the coming of that same Spirit, in order that the Church, the Body of her Son, might be born on Pentecost. Through her faith and love, Mary's maternity reached out to include all the members of her Son's Mystical Body.

116 Her union with the risen Lord has added to Mary's motherhood of the Church a new effectiveness, as she shares in the everlasting intercession of our great High Priest. In calling Mary "Mother of the Church," we are reminded that she is also the Mother of unity, sharing her Son's desire and prayer that his body be truly one. It is encouraging to note that some members of other Christian Churches, for example, John Macquarrie, found in Pope Paul's title, Mother of the Church, a sign of ecumenical hope.[78]

117 The basic reason why Mary is Mother of the Church is that she is Mother of God, and the associate of Christ in His saving work. Another great reason is that the Mother of Jesus "shines as the model of virtues for the whole community of the elect."[79] As Pope Paul put it, "Jesus gave us Mary as our Mother, and proposed her as a model to be imitated."[80] The Mother of Jesus exemplified in her own life the beatitudes preached by her Son, and so the Church, in and through the many activities of its various members and vocations, rightly regards Mary, Mother of the Church, as the perfect model of the imitation of Christ.[81]

118 The role of the Holy Spirit in the life of Mary is especially pertinent to our time. Mary of the *Magnificat* is, after Jesus himself, the supreme New Testament example of one who is led by the Holy Spirit. Not only the *Magnificat,* but Mary's whole life was a song of love inspired by the Holy Spirit. "Led by the Holy Spirit, she devoted herself entirely to the mystery of man's redemption."[82] She brought forth Jesus by the power of the Spirit. So too, Jesus is brought forth and lives in us through the Spirit.

Mary and the Priesthood

119 All the members of the People of God share in the priesthood of Christ and join in the offering of the Eucharist. Nevertheless, there is a difference not only in degree, but in essence between the common priesthood of the faithful and the ministerial priesthood of those who have received Holy Orders.[83]

120 At ordination, "by the anointing of the Holy Spirit," the priest is "marked with a special character," and is "so configured to Christ the priest that he can act in the person of Christ the Head."[84] His distinct calling to be fellow worker with Christ bears a resemblance to Mary's unique association in the saving work of Jesus. Our Lady's relationship to Christ the eternal High Priest overflows into her spiritual motherhood of all priests in their call to holiness and ministry. As our Lady's *fiat* at the Annunciation was consummated in her total surrender to the Father's will at the foot of the cross, so too through Mary's inspiration and intercession the priest is offered the grace of Christ to give of himself, in union with the Eucharistic victim, for the salvation of his fellow-men.

121 In the Latin Rite, the priest freely accepts the solemn obligation of celibacy out of love for Christ. The spotless purity of Mary is a constant source of inspiration and strength to him in living his celibate life. Having sacrificed for the kingdom of God the natural right to marriage and a family of his own, he feels himself more closely bound to the Mother of the Savior for whose sake he has made this sacrifice. There will be inevitable loneliness in the life of the good priest, accepted out of love for the suffering Christ. The sorrowful mysteries of the rosary have special meaning to the priest as he walks with the Mother of Jesus along the way of the Cross.

122 In Mary, Mother of the Church, the priest has the model of his own devotion to her Son. He looks to her, the woman of faith, for that faith and charity which will make fruitful his own human sharing in the priesthood of the Savior. And as Mary was faithful to the end, so he too is confident that he will persevere in the work God began in him by his Ordination.

Mary and Religious Life

123 In a family where love rules, the mother has a special affection for each child. Mary, Mother of the Church, is universal mother. In the community of faith, religious men and women hold a special place, and for them also Mary is Mother and model in a particular way. These religious, who have consecrated their lives to the Church, know from experience the tension between their vocation of prayer and the demands of the apostolate. Mary was the perfect contemplative, totally committed to "the one thing necessary," yet fully attentive to the needs of others, e.g., Elizabeth, the Cana couple, the disciples praying for Pentecost.

124 The special vocation of religious is to bear witness to the kingdom of God, both present and to come, by living in the spirit of the three vows which they publicly profess in answer to the Savior's evangelical counsels. Religious give up great human goods: the control of their possessions, the joy and companionship of married life, and free disposition of their personal talents. Catholic people rightly understand that the giving up of such human experiences, out of a desire to follow Christ, does honor also to the Christian vocations of the laity and supplies strength to the rest of the Church.

125 Their vows put religious at the disposal of their brothers and sisters in the wider Christian family, both for an apostolate free from family ties and for total dedication to prayer for the Church and world by cloistered monks and nuns. The goal of religious life is the Christian ideal of love of God and neighbor, not only in our present time-conditioned existence, but as a sign to the world of eternal union with the risen Christ, to which all men are called.

126 Again, it is the loving faith of Mary that makes her a perfect model for the religious. She is the greatest among the "lowly and poor of the Lord," whose trust in Him brings the abundant harvest. Humanly speaking, her virginity seemed to exclude her maternity; yet God made her Mother of the Messiah. Her poverty seemed to exclude her Son from the Davidic inheritance; but Jesus was the promised "Son of David." Her humble circumstances left little choice but to accept what life brought; but her splendid obedience made her an associate of her Son's saving work.

127 Mary's life testified to the kingdom her Son preached, which was inaugurated by His death and resurrection and the sending of His Spirit. "Temple of the Holy Spirit,"[85] she continues to exercise a special influence on religious men and women today, whose lives proclaim that the risen Christ reigns, and that union with Him, now and forever, is man's true vocation.

128 The founders and other holy members of religious congregations, past and present, have shown by example that true devotion to the Mother of Jesus is an indispensable element in maturing in the life of Christ. Now, as throughout the history of the Church, religious women find special inspiration in the Virgin Mother of Jesus. To both cloistered nuns and the Sisters active in schools and hospitals and other works of mercy and service, Mary remains the model of following Jesus.

Mary and Family Life

129 What does "holy Mary" say to struggling humanity in a sinful world? How does the example of her virtues touch laymen and women in the pilgrim Church? In her faithful discipleship, her union with Christ, her openness to the Spirit, Mary stands in contrast to all the sin, all the evil in the world.

130 We say "Holy Mary, Mother of God, pray for us sinners, now and at the hour of our death," confessing that we have added to the evil in the world by our own sins, and asking God's forgiveness. Yet our prayer is filled with confidence. For we find strength for the "now" not only in the constant loving intercession of the Mother of God, but also in the memory of how our Lady of the gospels lived the life of faith. The Mother of Jesus is the great exemplar to the whole Church; but she is model also to each individual in the Church, at every stage of human life and in every particular Christian vocation. No one ever followed Jesus so well as Mary His Mother. No one can help us more, by her example and by her intercession.

131 What does Mary mean to today's family? Mother of the Holy Family at Nazareth, Mary is mother and queen of every Christian family. When Mary conceived and gave birth to Jesus, human motherhood reached its greatest achievement. From the time of the Annunciation, she was the living chalice of the Son of God made man. In the tradition of her people she recognized that God gives life and watches over its growth. "Just as you do not know the way of the wind or the mysteries of a woman with child, no more do you know the work of God who is behind it all" (Eccl 11:5; see also Ps 138 (139):13; 2 Mc 7:22).

132 Reverence for human life as sacred from the beginning is bound up with the correct understanding and use of sexual love. Abortion arouses in the Christian the same horror as the slaughter of the Innocents in St. Matthew's gospel. Defenders of unborn life do well to appeal to the first part of the Hail Mary. Elizabeth's words, "Blessed is the fruit of your womb," are true in a real sense of every unborn child.

133 God called Mary and Joseph to sublimate the consummation of their married love in exclusive dedication to the holy Child, conceived not by a human father but by the Holy Spirit. When Mary said to Gabriel, "How can this be since I do not know man?" (Lk 1:34), the angel told her of the virginal conception. Joseph received the same message in a dream. Christian tradition from early times has seen Saint Joseph as protector of the Christ Child and of his wife's consecrated virginity throughout their married life.

134 Christian marriage is a sign of the union between Christ and His Church. Man and wife in mutual love, and in the children they welcome from God and care for, are a witness to the world of love of God and of their fellow-men. The offering of the bride's bouquet at our Lady's statue is an American Catholic custom that invites the Blessed Virgin into the life of the newlyweds. The conjugal chastity of a holy marriage is an answer to the neo-pagan degradation of human sexuality by pornography and by the glorification of promiscuity, divorce and perversions. Parents and children will find renewed strength in the grace of Christ and in the example and assistance of the Blessed Virgin, model of perfect purity and of self-surrender to God and neighbor. Christ was "Man of Sorrows," tortured and executed for the sins of men. Mary was "Mother of Sorrows" sharing her Son's sufferings even to Calvary. But there were also the joyous years at Nazareth, as her Son grew to adulthood, and something of the happiness of the Holy Family comes through in the gospel preaching of Jesus with His tender examples from home life.

135 Because she is seen as the Mother of all the living, Mary is viewed properly as the guardian of the child in the womb, as well as of the child that enters this earth alive. More than any other person, the Blessed Mother understood that the beginning of human life is attributable to God's creative love, as well as to the parents' action. When God became man within Mary, the Incarnation began. When Mary accepted the message from the angel and the Holy Spirit overshadowed her, the Divine Word, the God-man began to live. Entrusted with this precious life of her Child, Mary loved it, and defended it against all dangers. She protected Jesus before and after He was born.

136 So too, the Blessed Mother protects human life today from the moment of conception through birth (the beginning of our pilgrimage of faith), until all mankind realizes its goal in the Beatific Vision. Abortion, the deliberate killing of an unborn fetus, is a heinous crime and a serious sin. We, the Catholic Bishops of the United States, denounce abortion as an affront to the human race, as an unspeakable crime and a serious sin. We call upon all people of good will who reverence life to join in a crusade to protect life on all levels. No court, no matter how prestigious, can make acceptable what is obviously totally opposed to the Law of God and the best interests of our society.

137 Mary is Queen of the home. As a woman of faith, she inspires all mothers to transmit the Christian faith to their children. In the setting of family love, children should learn free and loving obedience, inspired by Mary's obedience to God. Her example of concern for others, as shown at the wedding feast of Cana, will exercise its gentle influence. "He went down with them ... and was obedient to them ... (Jesus) progressed steadily in wisdom and age and grace before God and men" (Lk 2:51-52). This obedience of Jesus is emphasized throughout the New Testament: at Nazareth, throughout His ministry in which He sought only to do His Father's will, even unto death. The Gospel makes clear also Mary's obedience to the Law and to the traditional prayer life of her people. This is evident, for example, in her annual trip to Jerusalem for the Passover. Faithful to the Law of Moses, the holy couple brought Jesus to the temple, His Father's house, for the presentation. Such obedience was the flower of Mary's faith. Because of it, God found her worthy to be the Mother of His Son.

138 In her appearances during the public life, Mary showed the same generous response to the will of the Father made manifest in her Son. At the marriage feast of Cana, after her Son's mysterious reference to the "hour not yet come," Mary's reaction was to advise the waiters, "Do whatever he tells you" (Jn 2:5). Family love builds on the fourth Commandment, and in Jesus, Mary and Joseph, parents and children have a powerful example of obedience to the will of God.

139 Family prayer, in whatever form it takes—meal prayers, night prayers, the family rosary, attending Mass together—provides opportunities for prayer to the Blessed Virgin. Children forget many things when they grow up. They do not forget the manly piety of the father, the gentle devotion of the mother, and love of Jesus and Mary as the support of the home, in sorrow and in joy.

140 Here we may recall the words of the Joint Pastoral Letter of 1968, *Human Life in Our Day:* "Because of the primacy of the spiritual in all that makes for renewal, we give top priority to whatever may produce a sound 'family spirituality': family prayer, above all that which derives its content and spirit from the liturgy and other devotions, particularly the rosary." [86]

141 According to the Gospels, Christ showed an enlightened attitude toward women: in His conversation with the Samaritan woman at the well; in His friendship with Martha and Mary, especially in His defense of Mary's preference to listen to His words, rather than wait upon Him; in His behavior toward the Syrophenician woman with the sick daughter (Mk 7:29); and in His appearance as risen Lord to Mary Magdalene, whom He sends to announce the good news to His apostles. These incidents, interpreted in their cultural context, give us a basis for a genuine emancipation and liberation of womanhood.

142 The dignity which Christ's redemption won for all women was fulfilled uniquely in Mary as the model of all real feminine freedom. The Mother of Jesus is portrayed in the gospels as: *intelligent* (the Annunciation, "How can this be?"); *apostolic* (the visit to Elizabeth); *inquiring and contemplative* (the Child lost in the temple); *responsive and creative* (at Cana); *compassionate and courageous* (at Calvary); a woman of *great faith*. These implications in the lives of Jesus and Mary need to be elaborated into a sound theology on the role of Christian women in contemporary Church and society.

Mary and Youth

143 Young people, adolescents in particular, will find in Mary the totally unselfish person, the brave young woman who could face and accept the hidden future bound up with being Virgin Mother of the Messiah. According to the customs of her time and people, Mary was probably no more than 14 when her parents arranged her marriage, and Joseph probably about 18. God asked great things of them both and they responded to His call with dedicated love.

144 So too, many young people today are eager to make the world into a better place, where justice and peace and love will prevail. The great obstacles still remain human greed and selfishness, all the deadly sins that bring turmoil and agony to so many suffering human beings. The succession of wars that grow in horror as technology improves, the oppression of underprivileged people at home and abroad, the imbalance between rich and poor countries are evils that become even more intolerable, when men would seem to have such great potential and when modern communications have so shrunk the information world. Only God can change men's hearts; only with the help of His grace can the enemies of mankind be conquered. Only those men and women will make an impact on society and change the world for the better, who make themselves powerful, effective instruments of God by lives of faith, hope and love, giving themselves completely to God in order that in and through them He may accomplish His great designs.

Mary and Single Life

145 Mary is model also for women who live a single life in the world. This can be a true vocation from God, freely chosen under the inspiration of grace, bringing with it the fruits of joy, personal holiness and unselfish service of others. Many a young girl, on the death of her mother, has generously taken on herself the care of younger brothers and sisters to train them in the love of God. Others dedicate their lives to the service of their fellow-men as nurses, teachers and social workers. Many exercise an apostolate through personal example and influence, and through their work in Catholic lay organizations. All these devoted women share in the spiritual motherhood of the Mother of Jesus and, like her, find true happiness and fulfillment in doing God's will.

CONCLUSION

146 As we conclude these pastoral reflections on the Virgin Mary, Mother of Jesus and Mother of the Church, we commend our efforts to her loving protection. For we are deeply convinced that the correct appreciation of the "mystery of Mary" leads to deep and perfect understanding of the mystery of Christ and His Church. We have contemplated our Lady with joy, pondering her holiness, her generosity, her hope, her burning love, her wholehearted dedication in faith to the saving work of her Son. For we believe the Father gave her to us as a "model of virtues for the whole community of the elect." May her pilgrimage of faith strengthen us in our individual Christian vocations. May her loving desire that her Son's words be heeded hasten Christian unity. May her motherly intercession make us worthy of the promises of Christ.

Appendix
MARY'S PLACE IN AMERICAN CATHOLIC HISTORY

Devotion to the Mother of God is well illustrated in American history, from early explorations, through the colonial period and the founding of the Republic, soon to celebrate its bicentenary. Christopher Columbus' flagship was the *Santa Maria*. His successors planted the Christian cross with the Spanish flag across many territories that now fall within the United States. The names these pioneers gave to many cities in the South and West are an indication of their love of Mary. For example, they gave Los Angeles the full name *St. Mary Queen of the Angels of the Portiuncola*. When Menendez landed in Florida in 1565 and founded the city of St. Augustine, the oldest city in the United States, one of his first acts was to have the chaplain, Father Mendoza, offer Mass in honor of Our Lady's Nativity. *Our Lady of La Leche* is still venerated there. In New Mexico the conquistadores paid tribute to the greater and fairer *La Conquistadora*, brought to Santa Fe in 1625.

The French missionaries came from the north, down the St. Lawrence, and our maps still bear traces of their devotion to our Lady. Pere Marquette explored the Mississippi with Louis Joliet in 1673 and called it *River of the Immaculate Conception*. Before him St. Isaac Jogues (d. 1646) and his companions had brought the Christian faith and devotion to Mary to the region around the Great Lakes. Our Lady of the Martyrs' Shrine at Auriesville commemorates their witness.

The England of penal times was an unlikely point of origin for an American colony where religious toleration would prevail and Catholics could publicly profess their faith, even their devotion to St. Mary. Yet George Calvert, a convert to Catholicism and the first Lord Baltimore, was given a charter to found the crown colony of Maryland, where religious freedom would be guaranteed. When he died in 1632, his sons carried the project through. Their two ships, *The Ark* and *The Dove,* landed in Maryland (named for the queen), March 1634. Their Chaplain, Rev. Andrew White, S.J., recorded how the Catholics of the group consecrated the future colony to Our Lady of the Immaculate Conception. They called their first settlement and capital "St. Mary's City," and they named the Chesapeake "St. Mary's Bay."

A son of Maryland, John Carroll, was the first bishop of the new United States. Consecrated bishop in 1790 on the feast of the Assumption, he placed his newly founded diocese of Baltimore under the patronage of Mary. In his first pastoral in 1792, he wrote: "Having chosen Her the special patroness of this Diocese, you are placed, of course, under Her powerful protection and it becomes your duty to be careful to deserve its continuance by a zealous imitation of Her virtues, and reliance on Her motherly superintendence." The Cathedral of Baltimore, which Bishop Carroll began, was dedicated at its completion in honor of the Assumption of Our Lady.

The world-wide movement which resulted in the definition of the Immaculate Conception by Pius IX in 1854, had its influence on the American Church. The sixth provincial Council of Baltimore was held in 1846 under the presidency of Archbishop Samuel Eccleston, S.S., of Baltimore, with 23 of the country's 26 bishops in attendance. Their first decision (May 13, 1846) was to request the Holy See that Mary under the title of the Immaculate Conception be named patroness of the United States. This petition was granted by Pope Pius IX in the following year. In their pastoral of 1846 the bishops wrote: "We take this occasion, brethren, to communicate to you the determination, unanimously adopted by us, to place ourselves, and all entrusted to our charge throughout the United States under the special patronage of the holy Mother of God, whose Immaculate Conception is venerated by the piety of the faithful throughout the Catholic Church."

The example of devotion to Mary set by the pioneers led to a pattern among American Catholics. Cathedrals and churches and chapels too many to enumerate carry Mary's titles across the country. From St. Mary's Seminary, Baltimore, founded in 1791, to the present, the institutions of higher learning bearing Mary's name are manifold. *Notre Dame* and all its lovely variants have become titles for many institutions and for every sort of Catholic apostolic enterprise, e.g., Sodalities, Legion of Mary, and the Family Rosary, which has spread from America to all the world.

In 1913 Bishop Thomas J. Shahan, fourth rector of the Catholic University of America, suggested the building of a national shrine of the Immaculate .Conception. This, he hoped, would be "a large and beautiful church in honor of our Blessed Mother, erected by nationwide cooperation at the nation's capital . . . a great hymn in stone." Most of the crypt area and the foundations of the upper church were built by 1931. In 1954 work began on the upper church and was sufficiently well along to permit the solemn dedication on November 20, 1959. Since then much more has been done and the Shrine, open daily and the scene of many religious celebrations, is still being completed. Contributions of Catholics country-wide maintain the magnificent church, as their offerings paid for its building, in testimony to the place the Mother of God, Mary Immaculate, holds in the hearts and religious life of American Catholics. Along with the many Washington visitors, of all faiths, who visit "the Shrine," in touring the Capital City, more and more groups are coming on pilgrimage, even from distant dioceses, and focusing on Mary's Shrine as a place of prayer and inspiration.

From this brief survey it is evident that a loyal and loving devotion to our Lady has been, from the very beginning, an important part of American Catholicism. It is up to the American Catholics of today to cherish and to pass on to succeeding generations of Catholics this rich heritage of devotion to Mary, the Mother of God and Mother of the Church.

References

With a few exceptions, Scriptural quotations are from *The New American Bible*, of which there are many publishers and editions.

After the Sacred Scriptures, the most frequently quoted source is the Second Vatican Council of 1962-1965. The text of conciliar pronouncements used by the editors of this letter is that published jointly in New York in 1966, by the Guild Press, America Press, and the Association Press, as *The Documents of Vatican II*, edited by Walter M. Abbott, S.J. For reference purposes, the title of this source will be given as DVII. The conciliar document most frequently drawn upon is the Dogmatic Constitution on the Church, the Latin title of which is *Lumen Gentium*. For reference purposes, this text is given as DCC, followed by the number of the paragraph from which the quotation comes, and the page number of the Abbott edition. On the relatively few occasions on which reference is made to another conciliar document (e.g., the Constitution on the Sacred Liturgy) the title of the document is given in full. Scriptural references are given parenthetically immediately after the text; the abbreviations are those of *The New American Bible*. Other quotations are followed by a superior number directing the reader to these References.

The Introduction

[1] Pope Paul VI, Address of November 21, 1964. *The Pope Speaks*, X (1965) pp. 137-138
[2] *Ibid.*
[3] DCC n.63, Abbott 92
[4] *The Pope Speaks*, X (1965), p. 140

The Text

[1] DCC n.58, Abbott 89
[2] DCC n.55, Abbott 87
[3] DCC n.56, Abbott 88
[4] *Ibid.*
[5] DCC n 55, Abbott 87
[6] DCC n.53, Abbott 86
[7] DCC n.58, Abbott 89
[8] Pierre Benoit, O.P., *The Passion and Resurrection of Jesus Christ*. N.Y., Herder and Herder, 1969, p. 141
[9] Henry Wansbrough, "The Resurrection." *The Way*, xii:2 (April, 1972) p. 144
[10] DCC n.63, Abbott 92
[11] DCC n.53, Abbott 86
[12] DCC n.63, Abbott 92
[13] St. Irenaeus, *Adversus haereses*, lib. v, ch.xix, n.1. Migne, PG vii, col. 1175
[14] DCC n.56, Abbott 88
[15] *Ibid.*
[16] St. Irenaeus, *loc. cit.*

[17] St. Hippolytus, quoted in Gregory Dix, ed., *Treatise on the Apostolic Tradition.* N.Y., Macmillan, 1937, p. xxi, n. 15-16
[18] Joseph Ratzinger, *Introduction to Christianity.* N.Y., Herder and Herder, 1970, p. 211
[19] St. Jerome, "Against Helvidius." *Dogmatic and Polemical Works,* tr. and ed. by John N. Hritzu. Wash., The Catholic University of America Press, 1965 (The Fathers of the Church Series) vol. 53, p. 19
[20] DCC n.46, Abbott 77
[21] John Macquarrie, *Principles of Christian Theology.* N.Y., Scribner, 1966, p. 355
[22] DCC n:56. In this instance the translation is taken from *The Pope Speaks,* 10 (1965) p. 396
[23] Pope Pius IX, Bull *Ineffabilis Deus,* Dec. 8, 1854
[24] John Henry Newman, *Faith and Prejudice and Other Unpublished Essays,* ed. by C. S. Dessain. N.Y., Longmans, 1956, p. 88
[25] DCC n.56, Abbott 88
[26] DCC n.56, Abbott 87
[27] *Oxford Dictionary of the Christian Church,* ed. by F. L. Cross, art. "Immaculate Conception of BVM." London, Oxford, 1957, p. 681
[28] DVII, Constitution on the Sacred Liturgy, n.103, Abbott 168
[29] Pope Pius XII, Apostolic Constitution *Munificentissimus,* Nov. 1, 1950, AAS 42 (1950) p. 770
[30] *Oxford Dictionary of the Christian Church,* art. "Assumption of BVM," p. 97
[31] DCC n.59, Abbott 90
[32] DCC n.68, Abbott 95
[33] Archbishop Philip Pocock, "Pastoral Letter." *The Ecumenist,* ii (May-June 1964) p. 73
[34] This is the title of one of Newman's "Sermons to Mixed Congregations." Text in C. F. Harrold, ed., *Sermons and Discourses, 1830-1857.* N.Y., Longmans Green, 1949. p. 247
[35] St. Cyril of Alexandria. Denzinger, *Enchiridion,* 250-251
[36] DCC n.62, Abbott 92
[37] Pope Paul VI, *Mense Maio;* English translation in *The Pope Speaks,* vol. X, 3 (1965) p. 220.
[38] DCC n.60, Abbott 91
[39] Frederick Jelly, O.P., "Mary and the Eucharistic Liturgy." *Our Lady's Digest,* XXVII (May-June 1972) p. 21
[40] DVII, Decree on the Ministry and Life of Priests, n.18 Abbott 570
[41] DCC n.53, Abbott 86
[42] *Ibid.*
[43] St. Augustine, "De Sancta Virginitate." Engl. tr. by John McQuade, S.M. In *St. Augustine: Treatises on Marriage and Other Subjects,* ed. by Charles Wilcox and others. N.Y., Fathers of the Church, 1955, vol. 27, pp. 148-150, *passim*
[44] DCC n.64, Abbott 93
[45] DCC n.61, Abbott 91
[46] DCC n.65, Abbott 93. See also DVII, Decree on the Apostolate of the Laity, n.4, Abbott 495
[47] DVII, Constitution on the Sacred Liturgy, n.103, Abbott 168
[48] DCC n.66, Abbott 94
[49] *Ibid.*
[50] Leon Cardinal Suenens, "Mary and the World of Today." *L'Osservatore Romano,* English edition, June 15, 1972
[51] Abbott, 78-85
[52] Herbert McCabe, O.P. Editorial in *New Blackfriars,* vol. 52 (Nov. 1971) p. 482
[53] DCC n.49, Abbott 81

54 DCC n.51, Abbott 84
55 *Ibid.*
56 DVII, Constitution on the Sacred Liturgy, n.8, Abbott 141
57 Eucharistic Prayer I
58 DCC n.68, Abbott 95
59 *Ibid.*, Abbott 96
60 Abbott, 94-95
61 DCC n.50, Abbott 83
62 Donald Attwater, ed. *A Dictionary of Mariology.* N.Y., Kenedy, 1956. p. 279
63 DVII, Constitution on the Sacred Liturgy, n.13, Abbott 143
64 DCC n.67, Abbott 94-95
65 *Ibid.*
66 Max Thurian, *Mary, Mother of the Lord, Figure of the Church.* London, Faith Press, 1963. N.Y., Herder and Herder, 1964, with title *Mary, Mother of all Christians*
67 DCC n.67, Abbott 95
68 Karl Barth, *Church Dogmatics.* London, Allenson, 1936, vol. 1, part 2, page 143
69 DVII, Decree on Ecumenism, n.11, Abbott 354
70 *op. cit.*, n.20, Abbott 362
71 Donal Flanagan, "Mary in the Ecumenical Discussion," *Irish Theological Quarterly*, vol. XL, July, 1973, pp. 227-249
72 Yves Congar, O.P. *Christ, Mary and the Church.* Westminster, Maryland, 1957
73 Flanagan, *op. cit.*
74 DCC n.52, Abbott 85
75 Macquarrie, *op. cit.*, p. 122
76 Pope Paul VI, Address of February 2, 1965. *The Pope Speaks*, X (1965) p. 103
77 DCC n.55, Abbott 87
78 Macquarrie, *op. cit.*, p. 122
79 DCC n.65, Abbott 93
80 Pope Paul VI, "Mary, Mother of the Church," May 13, 1967. *The Pope Speaks*, XII (1967) p. 285
81 Pope Paul VI, Address of Nov. 21, 1964. *The Pope Speaks*, X (1965) p. 139
82 DVII, Decree on the Ministry and Life of Priests, n.18, Abbott 570
83 DCC n.10, Abbott 27
84 DVII, Decree on the Ministry and Life of Priests, n.2, Abbott 535
85 DCC n.53, Abbott 86
86 Pastoral Letter *Human Life in Our Day.* In *Pastoral Letters of the American Hierarchy, 1792-1970*, ed. by Hugh J. Nolan. Huntington, Ind., Our Sunday Visitor Press, 1972, pp. 679-705

Suggested Readings

1. Commentary on the Marian chapter of the dogmatic constitution on the Church: by Donal Flanagan, in the book edited by Kevin McNamara, *Vatican II: The Constitution on the Church,* Franciscan Herald Press, Chicago, 1968.

2. *Prayers and Devotions from Pope John XXIII,* edited by J. B. Donnelly, Doubleday Image Paperback, Garden City, N.Y., 1969.

3. F.-M. Braun, O.P., *Mother of God's People,* Alba House, Staten Island, N.Y., 1967.

4. Raymond E. Brown, S.S., *The Virginal Conception and Bodily Resurrection of Jesus,* Paulist Press, New York, 1973, paperback.

5. Lucien Deiss, C.S.Sp., *Daughter of Sion,* Liturgical Press, Collegeville, Minn., 1972.

6. A. Gelin, S.S., *The Poor of Yahweh,* Liturgical Press, Collegeville, Minn., 1967, paperback.

7. Henri de Lubac, S.J., *Splendour of the Church,* Paulist, New York, 1963, paperback: chapter, The Church and Our Lady; also the pages on our Lady in "Lumen Gentium and the Fathers," in his book, *The Church: Paradox and Mystery,* Alba House, Staten Island, N.Y., 1969.

8. Heiko Oberman, *The Virgin Mary in Evangelical Perspective,* with preface by Thomas F. O'Meara, O.P., a Facet paperback, Fortress Press, Philadelphia, 1971.

9. Karl Rahner, S.J., *Mary Mother of the Lord,* Herder and Herder, N.Y., 1963.

10. Joseph Ratzinger, *Introduction to Christianity,* Herder and Herder, N.Y., 1970: chapter on "Conceived by the Holy Ghost, born of the Virgin Mary."

11. Edward Schillebeeckx, O.P., *Mary Mother of the Redemption,* Sheed and Ward, N.Y., 1965.

12. Max Thurian, *Mary, Mother of All Christians,* Herder and Herder, N.Y., 1964; the American edition is out-of-print, but the book can still be had under the title, *Mary Mother of the Lord Figure of the Church,* Faith Press, 7 Tufton Street, London SW 1, England.

STUDY QUESTIONS
Chapter One

1. What was the purpose of the American Bishops in publishing this Pastoral Letter on our Lady? Has devotion to Mary and the saints declined in recent years? If so, what is the cause?

2. Some say: "Today we should leave aside questions of doctrine and concentrate on an effective program for the social betterment of mankind." What do you think of this point of view?

3. Can the ills of society be cured by human efforts alone? To what extent is the help of God necessary to enable men to overcome their natural selfishness?

4. At Fatima, our Lady showed a deep concern for the state of the modern world. How does the example and intercession of Mary relate to the spiritual and temporal betterment of the world today?

5. What do the Bishops mean by declaring that Mary, the Mother of Jesus, has a special place in God's plan for the salvation of mankind?

6. Did Vatican Council II downgrade devotion to Mary? How has such an impression been created? Read chapter eight of the *Constitution on the Church* and discuss the attitude toward our Lady which is presented there. What have Pope John XXIII and Pope Paul VI said on this matter?

7. Protestants sometimes object that Catholic devotion to Mary is an obstacle to the knowledge and love of Jesus Christ. Is this accusation true? Show how devotion to Mary leads to a more profound knowledge and love of Christ.

8. The first chapter of the Pastoral Letter studies the various references to Mary in the Bible. Which passages are the most important?

9. Why is our Lady called "The New Eve"? Compare the role of Eve and of Mary in salvation history. Why is Jesus called "The New Adam"?

10. In the liturgy, the Old Testament passages referring to the "Daughter of Zion" are frequently applied to Mary. What did this term mean in the Old Testament? How is it applied to Mary by the New Testament writers and by the Church?

11. Read the description of the ark of the Covenant in Exodus 40:16-35, and explain the influence of this theme on St. Luke's descrip-

tion of the Annunciation and the Visitation. Compare, likewise, the account of the Annunciation with the promise to Abraham regarding the birth of Isaac.

12. What qualities of Mary's mind and heart are manifested in the account of the wedding feast at Cana? Would Jesus have worked this miracle if Mary had not asked Him to? What does this tell us about the place of Mary's intercession in our relations with Christ?

13. Christians through the ages have had great devotion to "the Mother of Sorrows." In what sense can Mary be said to have cooperated in the redemption of mankind and become the spiritual Mother of all those redeemed by her Son?

Chapter Two

1. Trace the chief points in the development of the Church's understanding of the mystery of Mary, as outlined in the first two paragraphs of this chapter.

2. Which points of comparison between Mary and Eve were emphasized by the early Fathers of the Church?

3. What is the difference between the Immaculate Conception and the Virgin birth?

4. Does the Church believe that the Virgin birth was a factual reality, or merely a literary device to bring out the importance of Jesus? What Scriptural evidence do we have on this point? What was the testimony of the early writers of the Church? What has been the constant teaching of the Church on the perpetual virginity of Mary?

5. In a number of places, the New Testament mentions "the brothers of the Lord." Does this mean that Mary had other children besides Jesus?

6. Show how Christian veneration of Mary is a fulfillment of her inspired prophecy: "All generations will call me blessed."

7. In what way is Mary blessed? Show the relationship between the external blessedness of Mary as Mother of Jesus and her internal holiness.

8. Explain the doctrine of the Immaculate Conception. Does this mean that Mary did not have a father or mother? Some medieval theologians found difficulty in accepting the doctrine of the Immaculate Conception because this seemed to them to free Mary from the need of redemption by Christ. How has the Church found an answer to this problem?

9. Explain the doctrine of the Assumption. Did Pope Pius XII make up this doctrine, or merely proclaim the historic belief of the Church?

Trace the history of the doctrine of the Assumption in the liturgy and the early Christian writings. How does Mary's Assumption serve as a symbol of Christian hope for the whole Church of God?

10. Some Protestants object to calling Mary "Mother of God." How would you explain this term to them? How is the divine maternity of Mary related to the doctrine of the Incarnation? Explain the controversies on this matter in the early Church and the solution arrived at in the Council of Ephesus, 431 A.D.

Chapter Three

1. The point is made that Vatican Council II only once used the term "mediatrix." To what extent was this an ecumenical gesture? Does the mediation of Mary in any way lessen our belief in the complete mediation of Christ? How has Jesus allowed Mary, and indeed all of the faithful, to share in His saving mission?

2. Catholics call Mary "our blessed Mother." Mary is clearly the Mother of Jesus; but how is she also our Mother? In what way is the spiritual motherhood of Mary the model of the spiritual motherhood of the Church?

3. What are the qualities of a good mother? To what extent are Catholics justified in believing that Mary manifests such motherly qualities toward her spiritual children?

4. To the woman who called His Mother blessed, Jesus replied: "More blessed are they who hear the Word of God and keep it." What did Jesus mean by this?

Chapter Four

1. What is the communion of saints? Is there a bond between the Church on earth, the souls in purgatory, and the saints in heaven? Explain how the divine life of grace, won for us by Christ, pervades all the members of His Mystical Body.

2. What is meant by "intercession"? Show how Catholic belief in the intercession of the saints implies that the saints know us, are interested in us, and pray for us. Read the appropriate passages in the seventh chapter of the *Constitution on the Church*.

3. Discuss the statement: "We seek from the saints 'example in their way of life, fellowship in their communion, and aid by their intercession.'"

4. Many pictures of Mary, such as that of Our Lady of Perpetual Help, had their origin among Catholics of the Eastern Rites. Can you tell anything of the devotion of Eastern Catholics to our Lady?

5. Discuss the practical suggestions in numbers 66-67 of chapter 8 of the *Constitution on the Church*. How can we, following the lead of the liturgy, cultivate devotion to Mary in our daily lives?

6. Do you think that some Catholics have gone too far in removing statues and pictures of Mary and the saints from the churches?

7. Is the rosary out-of-date? Too repetitive? Too impersonal? Explain how meditation on the mysteries should be woven into the recitation of the prayers of the rosary. Name the 15 mysteries.

8. Are Catholics obliged to believe in the apparitions of our Lady at Lourdes and Fatima? What kind of approval does the Church give to such apparitions?

9. Tell briefly the story of the appearances of our blessed Mother at Lourdes and Fatima.

10. What did Vatican Council II mean by advising us to avoid excessive sentimentality and vain credulity in our devotion to Mary?

11. What is the attitude of the Protestants you know toward Mary? How would you explain to a Protestant why we pray to the blessed Virgin?

Chapter Five

1. What is meant by the title "Mother of the Church"? What was the relationship of Mary to the Church during the life of Christ and after His Resurrection and Ascension?

2. How do all the members of the People of God share in the priesthood of Christ? Explain the difference between the common priesthood of the faithful and the ministerial priesthood of those in Holy Orders. What special powers are given to the priest at the time of ordination?

3. How can the example of Mary help a priest to be faithful to his vows and to his apostolate?

4. Name some of the chief religious orders in the Church and the work which they perform. Bring out various ways in which the example of Mary can aid religious in fidelity to their vows of poverty, chastity and obedience and help them in their work for God.

5. What was the secret of Mary's holiness, since her daily life at Nazareth was mainly concerned with little tasks, like sweeping the floor, cooking the meals, mending clothes and drawing water from the village well? How can Mary's example be applied to the work of a housewife and mother today?

6. Discuss the problem of abortion in the light of Mary's motherhood and her realization of the sacredness of human life. In what

sense are Elizabeth's words, "blessed is the fruit of your womb," true of every unborn child?

7. What reasonable precautions must an expectant mother take to preserve the life of her unborn child? Where can proper instruction on prenatal care be procured in your community?

8. On what points do you think an expectant father should be instructed during the time of his wife's pregnancy?

9. Maria says: "I have all my children baptized when they are eight months old." How soon after birth should a child be brought to the church for Baptism?

10. What provision should be made for the Baptism of the fetus in case of miscarriage?

11. What are the duties of parents with regard to their children's religious instruction? Should parents insist that children attend Mass on Sunday? What example should parents give to their children in this matter?

12. How can the religious education of preschool children be best promoted? What problems and difficulties are met with in introducing religious ideas to children below the age of six?

13. Outline an ideal program for family prayer. How much of this ideal can actually be put in practice in the average home? Does your family say the rosary together?

14. Is the Catholic attitude toward Mary an obstacle to women's liberation? To what extent has the Church's veneration of Mary lifted the status of women through the centuries?

15. What is the attitude of young Catholics today toward the blessed Virgin Mary? How can Mary be best presented to them as the model of unselfishness, courage, purity, and dedicated love of God and their fellow-man?

16. Are older single persons necessarily frustrated and unhappy? Explain how the single life in the world can be for some a true vocation from God, bringing joy and happiness in the unselfish service of others. Show how such persons can share in the spiritual motherhood of Mary and find in her a model of holiness.